Tyne & Wear Vol II
Edited by Angela Fairbrace

First published in Great Britain in 2007 by:
Young Writers
Remus House
Coltsfoot Drive
Peterborough
PE2 9JX
Telephone: 01733 890066
Website: www.youngwriters.co.uk

All Rights Reserved

© *Copyright Contributors 2006*

SB ISBN 978-1 84602 771 0

Foreword

Young Writers was established in 1991 and has been passionately devoted to the promotion of reading and writing in children and young adults ever since. The quest continues today. Young Writers remains as committed to the nurturing of poetic and literary talent as ever.

This year's Young Writers competition has proven as vibrant and dynamic as ever and we are delighted to present a showcase of the best poetry from across the UK and in some cases overseas. Each poem has been selected from a wealth of *A Pocketful Of Rhyme* entries before ultimately being published in this, our fourteenth primary school poetry series.

Once again, we have been supremely impressed by the overall quality of the entries we have received. The imagination, energy and creativity which has gone into each young writer's entry made choosing the poems a challenging and often difficult but ultimately hugely rewarding task - the general high standard of the work submitted ensured this opportunity to bring their poetry to a larger appreciative audience.

We sincerely hope you are pleased with this final collection and that you will enjoy *A Pocketful Of Rhyme Tyne & Wear Vol II* for many years to come.

Contents

Crookhill Primary School
Rebecca Young (10)	1
Amber Marrs (10)	1
Emily Moss (10)	2
Rachel Gardner (10)	2
Bethany Metcalf (10)	3
Adam Kelly (10)	3

Hetton Primary School
Paige Waters (9)	3
Jay Keiran James Batey (8)	4
Kaitlyn Ball (9)	4
Lauren Bolton (8)	4
Ryan Clark (8)	5
David Alcock (8)	5
Bradley Richardson (9)	5
Lianne Curle (9)	6
Jason Freeman (8)	6
Aaron Grievson (9)	6

Highfield Community Primary School
Ryan Hume (9)	7
Ellie Winston (10)	7
Amy Willoughby (9)	7
Jennifer Dodd (10)	8
Lauren Hill (9)	9
Ethan Bilclough (9)	10
Jordan Roof (10)	10
Callum Manchester (9)	10
Codi Herron (9)	11
David Kilpatrick (10)	11
Connor Carr (9)	11
Michael Carter (9)	12
Demi Thompson (10)	12

Roman Road Primary School
Harry Robinson (10)	12
Anna Candlish (11)	13

Phillip Scott (9)	13
Adam Barker (11)	14
Amber Smith (10)	14
Melissa Stokoe (10)	14
Ellisa Thompson (10)	15
James Bunn (9)	15
Kerry Woodhouse (10)	15
Thomas Little (8)	16
Liam Hall (9)	16

St Paul's CE Primary School, Sunderland

Karl Smyth (7)	17
Liam Hardy (8)	17
Gillian Butler (7)	17
Hannah Forrest (7)	18
Holly Falkner (7)	18
David Telfer (8)	18
Abbey Callaghan (7)	19
Adam Gibson (8)	19
Tamzin Robson (7)	19
Ethan Barber (7)	20
Olivia Ord (7)	20
Nikita Tsaliki (7)	21
Alisha Ruddock (7)	21

Sea View Primary School

Hannah Bailey (10)	22
Kayleigh Anne Gatenby (9)	22
Natallie Smith (9)	23
Darren Powell (10)	23
Sophie Lincoln (10)	23
Leigh Tampin (10)	24
Jac Clayton (9)	24
Skye Smith (9)	24
Alexander Cousins (9)	25
Carl Borthwick (9)	25
Ashley Cramman (9)	25
Reece Newman (9)	26
Jacob Porter (9)	26
Jon Ridley (9)	26
Ibrahim Mohiddin (10)	27

Kathryn Shaw (9)	27
Peter Higgins (9)	28
Caitlin Davison & Shannon Hale (9)	28
Liam Hall (9)	29
Ben Blackwell (10)	29
Rachael Luther (10) & Lauren Pearson (9)	29
Courtney Paul (9)	30
Ruby Bridgewood (9)	30
William Newton (10)	30
Georgia Lane (9)	31
Karan Isaac (9)	31
Jordan Telford (9)	31
Connor Olsen (9)	32
Daniel Pybus (9)	32
Scott Phinn (10)	33
Callum Gowman (9)	33
Hollie Wilkinson (10)	34
Chloe Emmerson (9)	34
Steven Hall (9)	35

Temple Park Junior School

Charlotte Thorpe (9)	35
Dean Beckingham (9)	35
Jazmine Stewart (10)	36
Rachael Slater (9)	36
Shannen Whittleton (10)	37
Lauren Roberts (10)	37
Bethany Collins (10)	38
Lindsay Marshall (10)	38
Kate Fairhurst (11)	39
Samuel Bell (9)	39
Laura Slesser (11)	40
Kayla McLachlan (7)	40
Alex Bruce (10)	41
Shaun Galloway (10)	41
Ellie Anderson (10)	42
Chloe Storey (7)	42
Lily Moore (10)	43
Ellis Lowdon (7)	43
Amy Cooper (10)	44
Abbie Dixon (10)	44

Jack Hearfield (9)   45
Robbie Woodmass (9)   45
Katie McArthur (10)   45
Kallum Emmerson (10)   46
Jordan Carter (10)   46
Rachel Barry (10)   47
Kaine Jackson (9)   47
Ellen Fail (9)   48
Chloe Scott (9)   48
James Dance (7)   49

Valley Gardens Middle School
Ben McDine (9)   49
Oliver Storey (9)   50
Andrew Parr (10)   50
Jessica Brown (9)   51
Lucy Carr (9)   51
Elliot Rogers (9)   52
Tom Wilson (9)   52
Victoria Wilkinson (9)   53
Robert Dean (10)   53
Chloe Rogers (9)   54
Lydia Ruddick (9)   54
Joe Foreman (9)   55
Jolene McIntyre (9)   55
Jenny Mills (9)   56
Nina Dungworth (9)   57
Daniel Simpson (9)   58
Robert Ferry (9)   58
Sam Thompson (9)   59
William McPherson (9)   59
Tom Scott (9)   60
Jamie Farnworth (9)   61
Rebecca McGarry (9)   62
Jessica Ivison (9)   62
Sarah Glendinning (9)   63
David Wilson (9)   63
Sean Findlay (10)   64
Joseph Robson (9)   64
Scott Rutherford (10)   65
Luke Beattie (9)   65

Adam Shorthouse (9)	66
Courtney Ward (9)	66
Edward Thompson (9)	67
Max Emery (9)	67
Thomas Sherreard (9)	68
Bethany Wilson (9)	68
Sofia Birch (9)	69
Joshua Gribbin (9)	69
Lucy Sherburn (9)	70
Aoife Oliver (9)	70
Jamie Chenylle-Proctor (9)	71
Jamie Leighton (9)	71
Luke Stronach (9)	72
Johnny Cattell (10)	73
Emily Wright (9)	74
Madeleine Ord (9)	74
Beth Ramsay (9)	75
Robbie Potter (9)	75
Daniel McIntyre (9)	75
Aidan Walker (9)	76
Kristopher Nef (9)	76
Ella Reveley (9)	76
Dominic Widdas (10)	77
Madeline Duggan (9)	77
Thomas Wheeler (9)	78
Jack Cochrane (9)	78
Jennifer Guillan (10)	79
Callum Lake (9)	79
James Bradford (10)	80
Sally Earl (9)	81
Hannah Redhead (10)	82
Victoria Tong (10)	83
Aine Singleton (9)	84
Scott Wraith (9)	84
Lucy Olson (9)	85
Lorena Weepers (9)	85
Mark Blyth (9)	86
Laura Milburn (9)	87
Louise Russell (9)	88
Cameron Barlow (9)	89
Liam Gunning (9)	90
Katherine Bradley (9)	90

Adrienne Lake (9)	91
Matthew Robson (9)	91
Andrew Bassett (9)	92
Jenny Ross (9)	92
Callum Preston (9)	93
Charlotte Barron (10)	93
Amy Bain (9)	94
Ross Murray (9)	95
Rachael Thornton (9)	96
Emily Davey (10)	97
Saoirse Stephenson-Lowe (9)	98
Jedd Burrough (9)	98
James Burt (9)	99
Hannah Tompkins (9)	99
Bradley Smith (9)	100
Lucy Richards (10)	100
Lucy Bruce (9)	101
Elliot Ross (9)	101
Katherine Russell (9)	102
Amy Fraser (9)	102
Ailsa Ingham (9)	103
Sarah Hamilton (9)	103
Heather McQuade (9)	104
Kasha Korzonek (9)	104
Liam Marriott (9)	105
Georgia Sturrock (10)	105
Josh Cogdon (9)	106
Max Graham (10)	106
Beth Richardson (9)	107
Oliver Spencer	107
Abbie Carr (9)	108
Daniel Robertson (9)	108
Johnathon Taylor (10)	109
Laura Campbell (10)	109
Imogen Green (9)	110
Dulcie Graham (9)	111
Drew Ellen Powell (10)	112
Caroline Taylor (9)	112
James Rowat (9)	113
Ryan Bird (9)	113
James Robson (9)	114
Andrew Taylor (10)	114

Patrick Maloney (9)	115
Sophie Hopkins (9)	115
Thomas Hoare (9)	116
Eve Beston (9)	116
Tobias Mill (9)	117
James Glendinning (9)	117
Scott Mogey (9)	118
Hannah Kessler (9)	118
Danielle Rawson (9)	119
William Patterson (9)	119
Jonathan Thompson (9)	120
Ryan Malarkey (9)	120
Georgina Ross (9)	121
Ellie Harkins (9)	121

The Poems

Apple

Apple, shiny apple,
Up in the fruit tree,
Apple pie for my tea.

Apple, crunchy apple.
Lovely as can be,
Apple pie for my tea.

Apple, green apple
Perfect for me,
Apple pie for my tea.

Apple, red apple
Yuck, yuck, yuck
Apple pie for my tea

As you can see,
I love apples,
Apple pie for my tea.

Rebecca Young (10)
Crookhill Primary School

Riddle

My first is in cherry but not in berry,
My second is in Harry but not in Carrie,
My third is in race but not in chase,
My forth is in ice but not in face,
My fifth is in snake but not in case,
My sixth is in tea but not in pea,
My seventh is in me but not in you,
My eighth is in cat but not in dog,
My ninth is in sack but not in back.

What am I?
A: Christmas.

Amber Marrs (10)
Crookhill Primary School

My Magic Land

My magic land,
Is better than a rock band,
It's full of CDs,
It's full of TVs,
It's full of dogs,
It's full of chocs,
And everything you can eat,

There's swimming pools
And scary ghouls,
And no school,
Hooray,
Everyone has pets,
Everyone has bets,
And candyfloss trees everywhere.

All the rivers are full of chicks,
And full of ships,
The sun never goes down,
And everything is full of smoothies,
And ice cream clouds,
There's diving boards,
And everything is free,
There are no honeybees,
And best of all, my family.

Emily Moss (10)
Crookhill Primary School

My Grandma

My grandma is a cake baker,
She also is a smile maker,
Even though she is a nutty singer,
She still is a fast knitter.
Once a week a bingo player,
Every month a crossword winner!

Rachel Gardner (10)
Crookhill Primary School

My Dog

Stick fetcher
Bone cruncher
Fast runner
Toy hugger
Rug ripper
Cat hater
House protector
Loud barker.

Bethany Metcalf (10)
Crookhill Primary School

Animal Alliteration

A ngry antelopes always argue,
N aughty newts are never non-aggressive.
I ntimidating iguanas always irk insects.
M anly mammals are mates with men,
A ggressive anacondas alarm all wrens,
L ittle lizards live with life,
S neaky snakes strangle with strife.

Adam Kelly (10)
Crookhill Primary School

Fear

Fear is grey like when you are walking down the street and there's
No lights on and somebody shouts your name and
You turn around and they scare you.

It feels spooky like a vampire.
It looks like a spooky, haunted castle.
It smells like an old witch dying.
It sounds like footsteps creeping up on me.
It tastes like a rotting dead body.
It reminds me of a vampire dying.

Paige Waters (9)
Hetton Primary School

The Ghostly Graveyard

In the graveyard where ghosts are exploring,
Going into shops and houses,
Making scary noises.
Moving and hiding stuff when we can't see,
Turning stuff on and off when nobody knows!
Secretly going into public places.
So if you hear a fearful noise,
Watch out, it could be a *ghost*.

Jay Keiran James Batey (8)
Hetton Primary School

Fear

Darkness is red like dripping blood.
It looks like a wine glass full of blood.
It tastes like crackling cat food.
It sounds like creeping footsteps.
It reminds me of my brother making me jump!
It feels like a ghoulish ghost behind me.

Kaitlyn Ball (9)
Hetton Primary School

Spooky

Spooky is black like a dark alley.
It feels scary like darkness all around you.
It looks like a dark alley with a stranger walking towards you!
It sounds like a girl screaming because a vampire bit her.
It smells like an ogre that is slimy.
It tastes like rotten cheese.
It reminds me of an old house that no one lives in.

Lauren Bolton (8)
Hetton Primary School

Spooky

Spooky is like a gigantic monster!
Spooky is black like night shadows!
It feels strange, like a monster biting you!
It sounds like a vampire creeping up on me!
It smells like a rotten witch that's dead!
It tastes like soaking sick in the bath!
It looks like a monster in the woods!
It reminds me of a witch whistling through the woods on her
                                                            broomstick!

Ryan Clark (8)
Hetton Primary School

Scary

Scary is like a big green ogre.
It feels spooky like a vampire biting into you.
It smells like a rotten body.
It tastes like soaking sick.
It looks like a massive monster.
It reminds me of my scary sister!

David Alcock (8)
Hetton Primary School

Scary

It looks slimy and horrible.
It is as scary as something long and hairy.
It sounds like an elephant creeping up the stairs.
It reminds me of a big giant.
It is the colour red and green.
It smells like an old man,
Who hasn't been in the bath for a year!

Bradley Richardson (9)
Hetton Primary School

Colours

Red and white dynamite.
Black and blue just for you.

Orange and gold makes you old.
Pink and purple is for a turtle.

Grey and green are so clean.
Burgundy and brown makes you frown.

Lianne Curle (9)
Hetton Primary School

Spooky

Spooky is dark like the night.
It feels like a vampire's cloak, and it is dark.
It sounds like a bat flapping his wicked wings.
It smells like some rotten stew.
It looks like a skeleton, bony and weak.
It tastes like slimy slugs, wiggling in the bowl.
It reminds me of an ugly wicked witch.

Jason Freeman (8)
Hetton Primary School

Scary

Scary is black and red like the night.
Scary reminds me of a dark alley.
Scary feels like gooey slime.
Scary looks like a garbage bin.
Scary sounds like a ghost whispering.
Scary tastes like a sizzling spider.
Scary looks like a wicked witch.

Aaron Grievson (9)
Hetton Primary School

Autumn Days

The smell of cut grass,
The lush taste of apple pie,
The trees start to die,
Hallowe'en is fun
Trick or treat, my favourite thing
Lots and lots of sweets.

Ryan Hume (9)
Highfield Community Primary School

Be Happy

B e near the fire.
E ggs from birds have grown.
H appily climb the monkey tree.
A n apple abandoned.
P eople pick purple PJs.
P ick the pink lipstick.
Y ou must love autumn!

Ellie Winston (10)
Highfield Community Primary School

Autumn

L eaves lying around,
E very leaf flying,
A mazing apples grow,
V ery large apples falling off the tree
E very bird flies away
S till birds stir.

Amy Willoughby (9)
Highfield Community Primary School

Alphabetical Animals

A wkward ambling antelope,
B rown bouncing bear,
C heeky chasing cat,
D aft dancing dog,
E xotic entertaining elephant,
F unny flying fish,
G reat giggling giraffe,
H eavy hopping horse,
I ll inviting iguana,
J olly jumping jaguar,
K ind knocking kangaroo,
L ong laughing lion,
M essy messaging monkey,
N aughty napping newt,
O ld organising owl,
P retty pushing pig,
Q ueer questioning quail,
R ough resting rabbit,
S melly snoring skunk,
T iny timid tortoise,
U gly upsetting unicorn,
V icious verifying vulture,
W ild wrestling whale,
eX citing X-raying X-ray fish,
Y ellow yawning yak,
Z ooming zapping zebra.

Jennifer Dodd (10)
Highfield Community Primary School

Alphabet Poem

A wkward ambling antelope
B ad bonny bat
C reepy clever cat
D izzy dancing dog
E normous electronic elephant
F luffy fat frog
G orgeous great giraffe
H ygienic hyper hyena
I ncy inside insect
J umpy jasper jaguar
K night knitting kitten
L azy Lizzie lizard
M oney-mental monkey
N oisy, noisy nurse shark
O range, orange octopus
P icky pink penguin
Q uick quicker quail
R ace racing rabbit
S ilver slow snake
T ongue twister tortoise
U mbro umbri umberelberbird
V ery void vulture
W iggle wonky whale
X enophobic xylophone X-ray bird
Y oung yonder yatchlizard
Z ealous zeal zebra.

Lauren Hill (9)
Highfield Community Primary School

Autumn

Autumn is pink like a pink rose
It tastes like a big yummy cake
It smells like a piece of fresh apple pie
I hear crunching leaves from the trees
I see happy people run in the crunching leaves
It feels like having hot chocolate
It sounds like a baby crying when you step on the leaves.

Ethan Bilclough (9)
Highfield Community Primary School

Autumn Days

Autumn days are great
The tastiest apple pie
As the bird flies by
Trick or treating more
The smell of leaves again, yeah
It's fun to see cows
It's fun to dress up like goats
Yellow leaves are bright.

Jordan Roof (10)
Highfield Community Primary School

Fun

Fun is blue like the sky on a bright sunny day
It looks like the smile of the sun
It sounds like someone laughing happily
It tastes like a jug of sugar

It reminds me of the time my dad did a handstand
And hit the light in the living room.
It feels like bouncing around on a trampoline
It smells like flowers in a field.

Callum Manchester (9)
Highfield Community Primary School

Autumn - Haiku

Autumn has conkers,
The leaves are any colour,
There are hollow trees.

Hallowe'en begins,
People dress up as witches,
They get sweets and treats.

You can smell cut grass,
You can step on crunching leaves,
And harvest begins.

Codi Herron (9)
Highfield Community Primary School

Silence

Silence is pale blue like the day's sky
It feels like a bronze statue.
It reminds me of when I sleep in my tent
It sounds like nothing.
It smells like a cold frosty morning.
It tastes like milk.
Its look is a 100-year-old tortoise.

David Kilpatrick (10)
Highfield Community Primary School

Autumn

I can feel the cold autumn wind hit my face,
I can see conkers on the ground,
I can hear the leaves rustle,
I can touch the hollow trees,
I can taste the sweet taste of biscuits,
I can smell the smell of cooking cakes,
I feel warm inside.

Connor Carr (9)
Highfield Community Primary School

Autumn

Crunching leaves fall down
On the ground, look over there
Red and yellow leaves

Robins in the sky
Robins singing in the air
Robins eating worms.

Michael Carter (9)
Highfield Community Primary School

Fun

Fun is like happiness and the colour of pink shiny lips,
It sounds like people sucking the water up in big gulps,
It sounds like friends running around beetroot-red,
It feels like soft creamy feathers tickling my toes,
It smells like flowers, sun, butterflies and things all happy around me,
It reminds me of exploding excitement.

Demi Thompson (10)
Highfield Community Primary School

Cry Of The Wolf

Wolf crying at the moon
Wolf coming very soon
Wolf creeping through the snow
Wolf, if you see it you've got to go

Seeking through the bushes
Crying in the night
Coming up behind you
It gives you a terrible fright

Walking in the forest
Looking for a clue
Coming really close then *chomp*
And that will be the end of you.

Harry Robinson (10)
Roman Road Primary School

Angels

Angels, angels have one lot of wings
Flying so high with golden rings
Flowers in their hair with eyes that gleam
Flowers that sparkle in the air.

Angels are wonderful in every way
With eyes that sparkle in the day
And then they shimmer in the light of May.

Angels are like feathers floating
Down from the sky.
Clouds in Heaven that fly so high.

Angels have trumpets and giggle a lot
With hands that touch you when you've got spots.

Angels are beautiful and very fair.

Anna Candlish (11)
Roman Road Primary School

What Is A Friend?

A friend is mint.
A friend is kind.
A friend will always be your mate.

A friend is cool.
A friend is fun.
A friend will always stick by you.

A friend is helpful.
A friend is fair.
A friend will always try to share.

A friend is nice.
A friend is funny.
A friend will always come to your birthday party.

Phillip Scott (9)
Roman Road Primary School

Roller Coasters

Roller coasters, roller coasters are so high.
I know one that can touch the sky.
When you go down one you start to scream
And then one moment your ears will steam.

Roller coasters, roller coasters are so much fun,
I know when it is going to go when I hear a gun,
Roller coasters have tight turns,
If it goes too fast I get burns.

Adam Barker (11)
Roman Road Primary School

Heaven

Heaven is like a field of flowers
It has got loads of powers
Fields of daffodils
Fields of daisies
Makes me feel like an angel passing by
In one flash from the sky.

Amber Smith (10)
Roman Road Primary School

Ignore Him!

It's dark and he's sitting on my chair!
Please help because he's just over there.
Ignore him! I tell myself, ignore him!
I can hear him scratching at the door,
Louder, louder, more and more
Ignore him! I tell myself. Ignore him!
I turn on the light and it flickers twice,
The truth is revealed, it's just my cat, Tice.

Melissa Stokoe (10)
Roman Road Primary School

The Wibberly Wobberly Monster

The wibberly, wobberly monster
Comes from outer space
He has spots all over his body
And spots all over his face.

He has stripes all over his fingers
And stripes all over his toes
If you look up close
You'll see his nose.
But you don't want to get too close!

Ellisa Thompson (10)
Roman Road Primary School

What Is A Friend?

A friend is kind.
A friend is cool.
A friend will always stick by you.

A friend is helpful.
A friend is true.
A friend will always be a good mate.

A friend is wonderful.
A friend will share.
A friend will always be the best.

James Bunn (9)
Roman Road Primary School

Happy

Happy feels like love in the air.
Happy tastes like ice cream.
Happy smells like red roses.
Happy sounds like Father Christmas.
Happy sounds like an angel's laughter.
Happy looks like golden stars.

Kerry Woodhouse (10)
Roman Road Primary School

What Is A Friend?

A friend is kind.
A friend is mint.
A friend will always be nice to you.

A friend is cool.
A friend is fun,
A friend will always make you laugh.

A friend is funny.
A friend is great.
A friend will always be your mate.

A friend is fun.
A friend is helpful.
A friend will always be good to you.

Thomas Little (8)
Roman Road Primary School

What Is A Friend?

A friend is good.
A friend is true.
A friend will always stick by you.

A friend is caring.
A friend is fun.
A friend will always be loyal.

A friend is kind.
A friend is your mate.
A friend will always be the best.

Liam Hall (9)
Roman Road Primary School

Smells

I like the smell of dark chocolate
I like the smell of oil
I like the smell of apple
I like the smell of soup
I like the smell of cake
But I don't like the smell of pillows.

Karl Smyth (7)
St Paul's CE Primary School, Sunderland

Smells

I like the smell of juicy apples
I like the smell of juicy fruit
I like the smell of kiwi fruit
I like the scent of juicy oranges
I like the scent of my dad's shiny car
I like the scent of my dad's aftershave
But I hate the smell of my dad's cigars.

Liam Hardy (8)
St Paul's CE Primary School, Sunderland

Smells

I like the smell of sweet, creamy pasta
Fresh from the oven,
I love the smell of sweet, creamy chocolate,
I love the smell of petrol
That makes my car go and
I hate the horrible smell of smoke!

Gillian Butler (7)
St Paul's CE Primary School, Sunderland

Smells

I like the smell of fruity gel pens,
I like the smell of flowers,
I like the scent of cakes straight out of the oven,
I like the aroma of juicy apples,
I like the smell of nuts
I do not like the smell of hamsters,
I do not like the fragrance of cats,
I do not like the perfume of cows,
I do not like the smell of bulls,
I do not like the smell of pigs.

Hannah Forrest (7)
St Paul's CE Primary School, Sunderland

Smells

I like the smell of coconut
I like the smell of brand new shoes.
I like the smell of doggy stuff.
I like the smell of perfume.
I like the smell of houses.
I don't like the smell of cheese.
I don't like the smell of horses.
I don't like the smell of hairdos.
I don't like the smell of pencils.
I don't like the smell of pigs.

Holly Falkner (7)
St Paul's CE Primary School, Sunderland

Smells

I like the smell of chocolate running down the spoon.
I like the smell of my dad's aftershave.
I like the smell of my dad's car.
I hate the smell of my mum's candles.

David Telfer (8)
St Paul's CE Primary School, Sunderland

Smells

I like the smell of a brand new book
I like the smell of a wall
I like the smell of some brand new shoes
I like the smell of some trousers
I like the smell of an exhaust pipe
I hate the smell of some petrol
I hate the smell of a car
I hate the smell of the wallpaper
I hate the smell of some paint
I hate the smell of a forest.

Abbey Callaghan (7)
St Paul's CE Primary School, Sunderland

Smells

I love the smell of apricot jam.
I love the sweet smell of honey.
I love the hot smell of popcorn.
I love the scent of burning toffee.
I hate the smell of my brother's feet.

Adam Gibson (8)
St Paul's CE Primary School, Sunderland

Happiness

Happiness is the colour of rosy red
Happiness is people cheering for joy
Red is the colour of devil eyes
Happiness is someone giving roses
But sadness is when my dog died.

Tamzin Robson (7)
St Paul's CE Primary School, Sunderland

Smells

I like the smell of warm runny chocolate,
I like the smell of juicy apples,
I like the smell of books,
I like the smell of white board pens
I like the smell of curry
And most of all I like the smell of
My dad's aftershave
I hate the smell of petrol
I hate the smell of rubbers
I hate the smell of stickers.

Ethan Barber (7)
St Paul's CE Primary School, Sunderland

The Scent Of Things

I love the smell of brand new tyres
On a brand new car.
I love the scent of
Brand new tennis balls
That come out of the tin.
I love the aroma of brand new sweets
That come out of the shops.
But most of all I love
The smell of my dad's aftershave.
I hate the whiff of eggs.
I really can't stand it!

Olivia Ord (7)
St Paul's CE Primary School, Sunderland

Smells

I like the smell of smooth chocolate.
I like the smell of strawberries.
I like the smell of sticky glue.
I like the smell of nice orange juice.
I like the smell of plastic.
I like the smell of my lovely mam's cooking.
I like the smell of healthy foods.
I like the smell of felt-tips.
I like the smell of the smooth paper of magazines.
I love the smell of red cherries.
I hate the smell of petrol.
I hate the smell of onions.
I have the smell of feet.
I hate the smell of smelly socks.
I hate the smell of sand.

Nikita Tsaliki (7)
St Paul's CE Primary School, Sunderland

Smells

I like the smell of my mam's perfume
I like the smell of a rose
I like the smell of a new cat
I like the smell of popcorn
I like the smell of strawberries
I don't like the smell of cheese
I don't like the smell of chicken
I don't like the smell of old books
I don't like the smell of fish.

Alisha Ruddock (7)
St Paul's CE Primary School, Sunderland

The Lighthouse

The lighthouse is the place to be,
With the smashing and the crashing of the stormy seas
Along by the tall, green, grassy leas.

The lighthouse is the place to be,
With the rocking boats down near the shore
Watch out, you might find an old shark's jaw.

The lighthouse is the place to be,
With the bright lights on you'll never lose your way
It guides the bobbing ships
As they swoop and dip over the waves
Towards the harbour.

Hannah Bailey (10)
Sea View Primary School

A School Day

A ll the children work hard

S omewhere where you can learn
C hildren play hopscotch in the yard
H appy teachers in the staffroom on a Friday
O r sitting at their desks drinking tea
O thers laugh and play around
L ots of stationery in their drawers

D inners are lovely in the dinner hall
A bsolutely the greatest friends
Y ellow walls in the corridors.

Kayleigh Anne Gatenby (9)
Sea View Primary School

Colours

Blue is like the glittering sky
Yellow is like the sparkle on a diamond
Red is the glistening in the Queen's crown
Black is like the darkness around us
Pink is rosy cheeks
Brown, the muddy footprints on the ground
Green is the stem on a rose.

Natallie Smith (9)
Sea View Primary School

Black Widows

Every day I walk to a beautiful hill
And I see this black widow that goes for the kill
It is black and fiercely still
If you were small and ran into it
It would be as heavy as a grill
The black widow has legs longer than a pill
And if it comes near me I'll show it
That people are brill.

Darren Powell (10)
Sea View Primary School

Sun, Sun

Sun, sun shimmering sun
Morning has come and your job has begun,
Your glistening light during the day
Makes me feel joyful and I want to play,
You look like a crystal gleaming and bright
Your blazing rays are an amazing sight
Your fantastic light that glistens and gleams
Oh sun, you're a marvellous sight to be seen.

Sophie Lincoln (10)
Sea View Primary School

The Sea

Waves are like an angry dog
Crashing on the shore.
It is very warm in the house
But people are disappointed for it is foggy outside.
The foghorn was booming loudly.
But then the fog cleared away.
No more crashing waves today.
People are coming out to play.
It has cleared away for another day.

Leigh Tampin (10)
Sea View Primary School

Pirate Ship

Pirates are evil and mad
Pirates can sail over stormy breaking waves
They find lots of treasure in deep dark caves
And kill many people because they are bad.

Pirates drink rum and eat salted fish
The captain gets whatever's his wish.
Pirates have swords made out of metal and wood
Pirates are part of an evil brotherhood.

Jac Clayton (9)
Sea View Primary School

Spook's Castle

It's as mysterious as night itself
Deep purple, mysterious and dark
Shivers and steals the night away.
It's like you're lying on a bed of nails
Creaks and groans like a phantom in the night
Deadly creaks, a ghost may wait
The sound of werewolves howling at the moon.

Skye Smith (9)
Sea View Primary School

Lego

Lego cars wheeling across the floor,
Just about to hit the bedroom door.
Bright coloured cars hitting the door,
I think I need a little bit more.
I think I need a lot more to build a tower,
That takes at least half an hour.
All that Lego built up high,
It could almost reach the sky.

Alexander Cousins (9)
Sea View Primary School

Tropical Island

There is an island in the middle of the sea
That everyone can see
Especially you and me.
They say there's a golden ball
In the middle of the Island of Hall
Whoever does get it
Is sure to regret it
And that's the story of the golden ball
That still is on the Island of Hall.

Carl Borthwick (9)
Sea View Primary School

Mansion Of Terror

Open the creepy door.
Walk across the cracked floor.
Look in the mirror, there's a ghost.
That means you're toast.
If you dare go near the handle.
You will get hit with a gigantic sandal.
If you lie on a bed of nails.
They will point in your back and you will be good as dead.

Ashley Cramman (9)
Sea View Primary School

Haunted Mansion

It's midnight in the mansion.
All the spooks are out and about.
If you go too near.
You will be in fear.

And if you open the door.
There is a wild roar.
And if you pass the wild boar
You get to face the executioner.

There is always a scream
Or a shout.
He always gets his prey
So beware.

Reece Newman (9)
Sea View Primary School

The Haunted Hotel

A ghostly, deadly, spooky place
Moving silently across the land,
Floorboards creak like madness,
Frightening danger lurks.
A shadow shoots swiftly.
Never go there alone.

Jacob Porter (9)
Sea View Primary School

The Scooter

As fast as the wind as it runs down the hill.
Grey as old car - reliable.
Fast as a bolt of lightning.
It pounds like a lion's roar.
It feels like you're on top of the world
Free, soaring like a bird.

Jon Ridley (9)
Sea View Primary School

Spooky Ball

Hello everybody, this is the haunted hall
Where witches and wizards have a wonderful ball
Mystic the cat and a witch called Peg
Are doing a jig with a wooden leg
But Peg the witch can't keep up with Mystic
'Cause her boots are too big and they tend to stick
The man who is dancing without one eye
He's eating the apple and stealing pie
There's a skeleton called Bone
Who's always talking to his friend on his phone
And the ghosts in the spectre band
With invisible instruments in their hands
Now it's time for you to go
But come back soon now you know
The secrets of the haunted hall!

Ibrahim Mohiddin (10)
Sea View Primary School

Autumn Conkers

Autumn, autumn all around.
Nice big conkers
Fall from the sky.
Onto leaves,
Making a bed on the ground,
All the boys and girls cheer,
Gather around to collect the goodies.
That are around.
Conkers squeal with delight
Scream and shout out loud.
It's conker season
Let the games begin.
Children challenge
Who will win?

Kathryn Shaw (9)
Sea View Primary School

Sea View Primary

S ea View Primary.
E xcited for each new day.
A maths lesson every day.

V iolin, guitar and brass lessons to do.
I like the teachers and the Head.
E specially like the new bike shed.
W orrying about not getting top grade.

P eople come from 5 to 11.
R eally cute 5 and 6 year-olds.
I love this school, I don't want to go.
M uttering in class to my friends.
A lovely playground too.
R eading, writing and arithmetic is taught.
Y eah, it is time for school.

Peter Higgins (9)
Sea View Primary School

Haunted House

Come inside.
On a spooky ride.
In the scariest house of all.
There's bats and ghosts,
Then you're toast,
In the creepiest castle of all.
Bring a light.
You may get a fright
As the mysterious black returns.
Your heart will be pounding.
Your eyes will be bloodshot.
As you enter,
The most creepiest castle on Moon Block.
So come on in!

Caitlin Davison & Shannon Hale (9)
Sea View Primary School

Pirates

Pirates' ships sail the sea
Horrible sounds of screaming
On board the wrecked ship
The sound of grinding bones
The shouting louder and louder
On board it is sleepy
Sound of cannons firing
The captain is happy and he shouts.

Liam Hall (9)
Sea View Primary School

Seasons Of The Earth

Spring is here, flowers bloom
While lovers start to meet and loom.
Summer has come so apples harden
Then fall to form nature's garden.
Now autumn has arrived, the leaves are golden brown
Now the floor is covered like nature's crown.
Now winter is present, it's icy cold
The flowers start to crisp and fold.

Ben Blackwell (10)
Sea View Primary School

Haunted Mansion

A scream of horror that sends a shiver down your back.
It's like a ghostly nightmare.
As black as the haunted night.
Whispers, creaks and creeps in the night.
A deadly phantom that beams in the midnight sky,
Like cold blood when you are sleeping
The darkest chocolate in the world.
The darkest jewel box in the darkest room of all.
The night of the haunted mansion!

Rachael Luther (10) & Lauren Pearson (9)
Sea View Primary School

The Haunted Castle

In the night, dark sky
As someone is whistling in the wind
In the night, dark, sparkling sky
Deep red for danger and death
As the darkness creeps so slowly
Someone is coming to walk in the distance and like a dark shadow
Pancake Jaffa syrup
Frightening dreams, dark, deep sleep.

Courtney Paul (9)
Sea View Primary School

The Sunshine

The sun is like a yellow ball bouncing around in the sky.
Sun is bright yellow like pollen inside a flower.
It glides and floats up and down.
It looks like a golden flower head.
It's a startling, shiny, shimmering dream.
It looks like a yellow, round, shiny, smooth apple.
It's like a beautiful bronze patchwork cloth.
It sounds like a peaceful breath of air.

Ruby Bridgewood (9)
Sea View Primary School

Dragon

The village is a-flame,
Because no one could take,
The dragon's awesome power,
In this unholy hour.
His name is Fire Drake,
And for your own sake,
Stay away from this unforgiving creature,
Unless you want to become a dinner feature.

William Newton (10)
Sea View Primary School

The Haunted Castle

The haunted castle is like a monster
Screaming people can be heard
It's velvet, purple, rich, dark and dangerous
It sways side to side hypnotising you.
Your worst nightmare, it haunts your dreams
Feeling, screaming and thrilling.

Georgia Lane (9)
Sea View Primary School

Bumblebee

B ee, bee
U are great
M aking honey all day
B ee, bee
L ending honey all day
E veryone has enough
B ee, bee
E xcellent bee
E very day, everywhere.

Karan Isaac (9)
Sea View Primary School

The Night

A swift shadow sneaks upon you.
It could only happen in the night.
Silently and swiftly a phantom steals the light.

When you walk through the deadly fog
It's like a bottomless bowl of soup.
Screams shatter the silence.
Inky grey covers the path
People are dreamless and scared
Until morning comes.

Jordan Telford (9)
Sea View Primary School

How To Treat A Bumblebee

High in the air flies the bumblebee.
It flies in the open
Open and free.
It stings
So do not disturb,
Is a bee a noun or a verb?
Unlike wasps
They are soft as silk
Their deaths are nigh
Just watch as they fly.

Connor Olsen (9)
Sea View Primary School

Haunted Being

Come inside
We won't lie
Someone is going to die
There are ghosts in the sky
Go in the attic
Do not panic
That's a safe place to be
Just as long as you don't mind our pet bee
Run far away
Before the end of the day
And enjoy your life.

Daniel Pybus (9)
Sea View Primary School

Panda's Life

Roaring fiercely if a trespasser comes near her baby
She is like a gorilla swinging across the branches of the oak trees
She is like a black and white old-fashioned film
Racing through the jungle as if a pack of lions is chasing her
Her appearance is a beast awoken from the dead
When she is free and away from death she is as chuffed
As a little boy getting a PS3
She is like a gigantic Swiss roll
She is as soft as a soft sofa
Munching on bamboo day after day, year after year.

Scott Phinn (10)
Sea View Primary School

Untitled

Sound of the wrestler's war
Tunes that make the crowd
Go wild, walk down the
Aisle taunting the crowds
A child steps into the ring
With a great big smile
Claps his hands and the crowd goes wild
He wins the match
The crowd clap
And then he returns back to class
Great, double maths.

Callum Gowman (9)
Sea View Primary School

School

I go to school five days a week,
I go there to learn.
I listen when the teachers speak,
And answer when it's my turn.

Straight after my dinner,
I go to piano class.
Since I am a beginner,
I have to have a pass.

It is nearly time for home,
It is three o'clock.
I am telling my mum I wrote a poem,
Which will give my mum a shock.

Hollie Wilkinson (10)
Sea View Primary School

The Castle On The Hill

A haunted castle on the hill.
A nice old man who said he's Bill
An owl that hoots and tweets
Upon an ancient wooden seat
A person weeps in the castle walls
A man falling dead from up high calls
A ghost cries and sighs alone
She's a little girl that's called Simone
The moon shines down without a sound
But there'll always be the sound of hearts that pound
The haunted castle on the hill.

Chloe Emmerson (9)
Sea View Primary School

Sharks

It looks like a sabre-toothed tiger
Staring at you
Black and white
Disguised in the darkness
Sharks are like a knife
Gliding through the water
As smooth as a new bought couch.
It waves its head side to side
In a scary way
Angry like a tiger.

Steven Hall (9)
Sea View Primary School

Rainbow

Rainbows are beautiful in every single way,
I love it how they can appear any day
Red, pink, orange and yellow,
These colours are quite mellow
They can appear any time in the sky,
I wonder why?

Charlotte Thorpe (9)
Temple Park Junior School

Red

Red is paint on the paper.
Red is on your cheeks when you are shy.
Red is when you cut your finger.
Red is a Tudor rose, redder than ever.
Red is the sun glowing very hot.

Dean Beckingham (9)
Temple Park Junior School

Names Of Friends

A is for Amy who has neat writing.
B is for Bethany who is so friendly.
C is for Callum who is so cool.
D is for Decon who has moved school.
E is for Ellie who is so kind to people.
F is for Fred who I don't know.
G is for Georgia who plays with me at home.
H is for Hannah who is always happy.
I is for Iain who is my friend in the street.
J is for Joy who is always funny.
K is for Katie who is my best friend.
L is for Lauren who is my friend as well.
M is for Mrs Palmer who is my best teacher.
N is for Nancy who is in hospital.
O is for others who you can be your friend.
P is for Peter who is my friend at home.
Q is for nobody but you might think of someone.
R is for Rachel who laughs a lot.
S is for Shaun who is so silly.
T is for Tom who is in Mrs Nixon's class.

Jazmine Stewart (10)
Temple Park Junior School

Hallowe'en

Hallowe'en, such a fright
Makes you bump through the night
Witches and ghouls all come after you
At midnight you hear voices saying, 'I'm coming to kill you!'
Then zombies come and carry you to the vampire's lair
After that the vampire takes a bite out of you
And guess what he says,
'Happy Hallowe'en!'

Rachael Slater (9)
Temple Park Junior School

Things About Me!

S is for special in every way
H is for happy on most days
A is for active as I like to dance
N is for naughty, but mostly I'm nice
N is for nasty but that's what I'm not
E is for easy-going because that's what I am
N is for noodles, one of my favourite foods

W is for wicked and that's my sense of humour
H is for helpful, that's what I try to be
I is for intelligent as that's what I hope to be
T is for trustworthy as you can always count on me
T is for trampolining as I have so much fun
L is for lion, my best animal of all
E is for exciting so that's just me, me, me
T is for terrified of those buzzy, buzzy bees
O is outstanding as I like this poem to be
N is for noisy as this I sometimes am.
   So that's just me!

Shannen Whittleton (10)
Temple Park Junior School

A Unicorn

Your mane so long
Your fur so silvery white
As you gracefully drink from the stream in the moonlight
Your eyes, dazzling, like the sun upon a stream you are a vision
People only see at night in their dreams
You are an enchanted creature
With an adorable face
Are you a horse from this world
Or a mythical place?

Lauren Roberts (10)
Temple Park Junior School

In The Haunted Castle

In the haunted castle,
Spooky things might happen,
Ghosts and witches,
Skeletons and mummies,
Watch out, they might get you.

In the haunted castle,
Spooky things might happen,
Chairs rocking,
Pianos playing,
All alone with no one there.

In the haunted castle,
Spooky things might happen,
Ghosts walking through you,
Skeletons and mummies awaking,
Sending shivers down your spine.

Bethany Collins (10)
Temple Park Junior School

Me And My Dreams

I dreamt that . . .
I was flying high up
Through the misty sky

I dreamt that . . .
I was in my world
Playing with my friends.

I dreamt that . . .
I was sitting on clouds
Minding my own business

I dreamt that . . .
I was with my family
Running through the air.

Lindsay Marshall (10)
Temple Park Junior School

Things About Me

A is for alive, I always am
B is for bright, lit up sometimes
C is for crazy, my friends say so
D is for dippy, sometimes I am
E is for excellent, I don't know if I am
F is for friends, I hope I am
G is for girl, girls do rule
H is for house captain, I got voted
I is for interesting, I sometimes am
J is for Jack-in-the-box, I am bouncy
K is for Kate, that's my name
L is for Laura, my best friend
M is for mates, I hope I have some
N is for necklace, I have loads
O is for outgoing, I hope I am
P is for perfect, that's what I am
Q is for quirky, I really am
R is for reading, I love to
S is for special, I don't think I am
T is for thinking, I really am trying
U is for useless, I hope I'm not
V is for vivid, I am sometimes
W is for wild, I'm like that sometimes
Y is for yippee, you've finished the poem.

Kate Fairhurst (11)
Temple Park Junior School

Today

Today, lotuses floating on wind
Today, river so calm
Today, blossom falls softly
Today, birds sing a sweet harmony
Today, the sky is orange and sweet.
Today is perfect
Will tomorrow be?

Samuel Bell (9)
Temple Park Junior School

Alphabet Poem

A is for athletic, which I am not
B is for brilliant, all my friends think I am
C is for cute, I certainly am
D is for delightful, I think I am
E is for excitable, my teacher thinks I am
F is for fun, I have lots of that
G is for good, I am a good worker at school
H is for helpful, my best friend thinks that I am
I is for incredible, my stories sometimes are
J is for June, that is my favourite time of year
K is for Kate, she is my best friend
L is for Laura, that is my name
M is for mysterious, my brother thinks I am
N is for nice, I think I am
O is for oranges, I absolutely hate them
P is for perfect, nobody is
Q is for quiet, no one thinks I am
R is for responsible, I really am
S is for super, I am not Superman
T is for trouble, I'm not
U is for unreal, I am not
V is for valentine, I do not have one
W is for wise, I think I am
X is for xylophone, I like playing with them
Y is for young, I am
Z is for zealous, I really am.

Laura Slesser (11)
Temple Park Junior School

My Dog Harvey

My dog Harvey loves to party
All through the night
When he walks he shakes his booty
And hopes he'll get a chocolate cookie.

Kayla McLachlan (7)
Temple Park Junior School

New Fern Friends

Oh little fern
All alone
What you
Need is
A nice
New home
Come with
Me to
A home
Of plenty
With lots
Of love
And attention
This is what
You'll get
At one
Hundred and
Twenty.

Alex Bruce (10)
Temple Park Junior School

My Dog Zena

My dog Zena, small and white
Although she barks at night.
She barks and barks and barks
Until the morning light.

She's out of bed in a shot
To see what we have got
She'll have her breakfast in a bowl
Then I take her for a stroll.

After the stroll we get back home
I get ready for school in a rush
And run along the road for my bus.

Shaun Galloway (10)
Temple Park Junior School

Finally

Walk through the school gate,
Yeah, can't wait.

In the classroom, sitting down,
The teacher comes in with a big frown.

Sitting doing hard work,
When will it end? Soon I hope.

The bell has rung, time for the first play,
Hooray!

Now we do more work, harder in fact,
Next week it's the SATs.

Dinnertime at last, there's a curse
At school a spell that's been cast.

Finally it's home time
Hooray! It's Friday.

Ellie Anderson (10)
Temple Park Junior School

Parrots

My pet parrot loves carrots.
His name is Fred.
His head is red.
He squeaks and squawks
When it's time for bed.

It's always late
When he gets up in the morning,
And all day long
He's yawning and yawning.

He sits in his cage,
In wait for his bait.
He goes in a rage,
Cos it's late, late, late.

Chloe Storey (7)
Temple Park Junior School

The Sea

Look!
Over there,
A fishing boat,
Bobbing up and down on the misty waters.

Look!
Over there,
A cool surfer,
Riding across the awesome waves.

Look!
Over there,
A seagull,
Gliding above the calm ocean.

Look!
Over there,
A majestic whale,
Breaking into the waves.

Lily Moore (10)
Temple Park Junior School

The Tooth Fairy

Is there really a tooth fairy?
Is her name Tinkerbell or maybe Mary?
What does she look like? No one knows.
She visits in summer and when it snows.

Does she have wings?
I'd like to see,
Just what happens when she visits me.
She leaves my 50p or a pound.
She must be invisible,
She doesn't make a sound.

Goodnight tooth fairy,
I'll see you soon,
Tinkerbell or Mary visiting my room.

Ellis Lowdon (7)
Temple Park Junior School

Nature's Gifts

Nature gives us everything,
Food, water and our clothes,
Our five senses come from it,
Eyes, mouth, ears, hands and nose.

Nature gives us everything,
Like wonderful sights to see,
From the smallest colourful butterfly,
To the great waves of the sea.

Nature gives us everything,
The precious stones we keep,
Like diamonds, emeralds, rubies too,
And pearls from the ocean deep.

Nature gives us everything,
It made us, me and you,
Skeleton, muscle, organ, nerve,
It gave us emotions too.

Nature gives us everything,
But what do we give back?
Greenhouse gases, pollution and fumes
And clouds of smoke that are thick and black.

Amy Cooper (10)
Temple Park Junior School

Playground

Out in the playground
Screaming and shouting
Out in the playground
Hopscotch counting

Bell rings
Let's go home
And this is the end
Of this poem.

Abbie Dixon (10)
Temple Park Junior School

Notes For A Summer Painting

Pale blue skies.
Flowers dance in the sun.
Children playing hopscotch.
Sunset glowing brightly.
Freshly cut pasture.
Animals bound with joy.
Church bells ring.
Butterflies flutter in the breeze.
Dragonflies float on the wind.
Skylarks swiftly soar.

Jack Hearfield (9)
Temple Park Junior School

Cars

I love cars, they are my passion.
I love them whatever their fashion.
They cannot go too fast for me,
Slowly doesn't bother me,
I just love cars.
Fast cars, slow cars,
Big cars, small cars,
Because cars are my passion.

Robbie Woodmass (9)
Temple Park Junior School

Colours

The sun is yellow.
The sky is blue.
Look at the colour of me and you
You are yellow.
I am blue.
You're a blossom, I am too!

Katie McArthur (10)
Temple Park Junior School

Deep Blue Sea

D eep under the sea where
E nchanting animals and plants live,
E verywhere you look it's blue, dark and mysterious
P lants are green, pink and all sorts of weird colours.

B ig, great predators live in the sea.
L ooking for prey, scavengers eat the leftovers.
U nder rocks live colourful crabs and
E arth's creatures evolved from the sea.

S harks are one of the many species.
E els, turtles, manta rays
A nd sea lions live close to the surface.

Kallum Emmerson (10)
Temple Park Junior School

Rain

It splashed and crashed on my head when I was walking through the rain.

The rain crashed and splashed all over my clothes when I made my way through the rain.

It crashed and flashed when I was running through the rain.

It smashed against the trees and fences when I was standing under the tree in the rain.

In the end I was just soaked when it crashed and smashed on me.

Jordan Carter (10)
Temple Park Junior School

The Night Creeper

Every evening, every night,
It creeps about giving you a fright.
It's big and green and covered in hair,
And its sharp claws will give your dad a scare.

It has ugly horns and wonky teeth,
Can it really be real nice underneath?
It'll smash your windows, rattle your door,
Repairing them isn't half a chore.

But remember friends, a cave is its lair,
So *do not* mistake it for a bear.
With its green leaf lamp and grassy beds,
Don't wake the night creeper,
It'll rip you to shreds!

Rachel Barry (10)
Temple Park Junior School

Fireworks

F ireworks are exciting.
I love the sound, *bang!*
R oaring through air, *boom.*
E veryone amazed.
W ow, look over there.
O oh it's freezing.
R ockets soar.
K aine loves them.
S parklers fizzle.

Kaine Jackson (9)
Temple Park Junior School

Top Shop

Hi there!
I can't decide what top to wear
I have,
Red tops, green tops,
Colours-in-between tops,
Dotty tops, spotty tops,
Really very weird tops,
School tops, crop tops,
Very, very, cool tops,
Black tops, white tops,
Ones that give you a fright tops!
I still haven't decided,
What would you pick?

Ellen Fail (9)
Temple Park Junior School

Hallowe'en

H airy and scary, the werewolf growls
A liens eerily scowling
L urking around, the witches scare
L ooking for blood to suck, everyone beware
O oooooooooooohhh! the ghouls chant
W eird noises, the Frankenstein pants
E erie aliens flying about
E choey screaming
N ew baby ghosts wickedly laughing but only dreaming!

Chloe Scott (9)
Temple Park Junior School

I Have A Fluffy Cat

I have a fluffy cat,
That sat on a mat.
She got chased by a dog,
And then she sat on a bumpy log.
She got very, very scared,
But stuck out her claws,
And hissed at the dog.
And the dog ran away.
The cat was happy now,
And she walked home.

James Dance (7)
Temple Park Junior School

Happiness And Sadness

Happiness
Happiness is like music flowing through your body.
It tastes like a Galaxy chocolate bar on your taste buds.
It sounds like a cute bird tweeting in the morning.
It smells like chocolate slowly melting.
It looks like a beautiful stream flowing.
It feels like animals' soft, cosy fur.

Sadness
Sadness is like a volcano erupting.
It tastes like a fireball going down in your mouth.
It sounds like a growl from a dog.
It smells like a fishpond all mouldy and green.
It looks like a rainy, wet cloud.
It feels like your heart is going to explode.

Ben McDine (9)
Valley Gardens Middle School

Happiness And Sadness

Happiness
Happiness is like having lots of reward time.
Happiness smells like freshly baked chocolate cake.
Happiness sounds like sweet blue tits in the midday sun.
Happiness feels like paradise.
Happiness tastes like Thorntons best, most delicious, hot and oozing, fantastic milk, white and dark chocolates with tasty moreish caramel squirting out the top when you bite into it!
Happiness looks like the fantastic forests and mountains of the world.

Sadness
Sadness is like Thorntons to be closed.
Sadness feels like having no pocket money.
Sadness smells like burnt sausages in a frying pan.
Sadness tastes like a horrible cold, getting stronger,
Cup of mouldy tea.
Sadness sounds like funeral music.
Sadness looks like a family dying, very, very, very ill in hospital.

Oliver Storey (9)
Valley Gardens Middle School

Sadness

It feels like sitting all alone at home.
It's like a rainy day.
It's like not seeing my friends and being poorly.
It's like having autism and not feeling special.
It's like being injured for a long time.
It's like having school trips cancelled.
It's like not being able to eat lovely fresh bread.
It's like somebody bullying me all day long.

Andrew Parr (10)
Valley Gardens Middle School

Emotions

Excitement is like butterflies sweeping.
Excitement tastes like hot treacle.
Excitement smells like cream.
Excitement looks like a bouncy ball flying.
Excitement feels like soft clouds.
Excitement sounds like springs jumping.

Boredom is grey.
Boredom tastes like blood.
Boredom smells like leaking gutters.
Boredom looks like dark paths.
Boredom feels like your heart turning cold.
Boredom sounds like clocks ticking loudly.

Jessica Brown (9)
Valley Gardens Middle School

Emotions

Happiness is yellow like the shining sun.
Happiness tastes as sweet as sugar.
Happiness feels as smooth as silk
Happiness looks like flowers swaying in the wind.
Happiness sounds like birds tweeting in the daylight.
Happiness smells like freshly cut grass.

Sadness is like a teardrop falling to the ground.
Sadness tastes as sour as a lemon.
Sadness feels as cold as ice.
Sadness sounds like the wind howling through the trees.
Sadness smells like an old deserted house.
Sadness looks like a damp, gloomy night.

Lucy Carr (9)
Valley Gardens Middle School

Happiness And Anger

Happiness
Happiness is as sweet as sour Haribos.
It smells like fresh doughnuts.
It tastes like creamy white Magnums.
It looks like big red fire engines.
It sounds like cheering on someone.
It feels like a nice, cosy, warm bed.

Anger
Anger is as red as a volcano erupting.
It smells like burning flames from a bonfire.
It tastes like extra-sour sweets.
It looks like a dark, wet, damp hole full of creepy-crawlies.
It sounds like people screaming and shouting.
It feels like scorching hot water.

Elliot Rogers (9)
Valley Gardens Middle School

Anger And Happiness

Anger
Anger is as dark as a dragon's insides.
It tastes like a batch of raw meat.
It looks like a dinosaur roaring ahead,
It smells like a pile of burning wood.
It feels like boiling flesh.
It is so terrible . . . it is anger.

Happiness
It tastes like a juicy green apple.
It smells like a fresh mint plant.
It feels like a dog's fur coat.
It looks like a sweet chocolate bar.
It is like the warm blue sky . . . it is happiness.

Tom Wilson (9)
Valley Gardens Middle School

Emotion Colours

Anger is blood red like a burning fire.
Anger is black like the night sky.
Anger is blue like the roaring sea.

Sadness is green like the swishing grass.
Sadness is white like a gleaming cloud.
Sadness is blue like a teardrop from your eye.

Happiness is yellow like the rising sun.
Happiness is pink like peace.
Happiness is orange like a piece of fruit.

Excitement is gold like a golden ring.
Excitement is silver like a silver ring.
Excitement is red like a piece of lava.

Depression is grey like a stormy sky.
Depression is white like a blank piece of paper.
Depression is brown like a tree stump.

Victoria Wilkinson (9)
Valley Gardens Middle School

Simile Poem

Anger is red like fierce blood
It smells like sour sprouts,
It tastes like too much chocolate.
It sounds like rude children laughing.
It feels like a different world.

Happiness is yellow like dancing dandelions.
It tastes like new fresh Coke.
It smells like sizzling bacon,
It sounds like singing birds,
It feels like a beautiful world.

Robert Dean (10)
Valley Gardens Middle School

Happiness And Anger

Happiness
Happiness is red like sweet juicy apples.
It tastes like sweet sugar.
It smells like chocolate-covered strawberries.
It looks like a garden of sweet-smelling roses.
It sounds like singing birds.
It feels like walking along a sunny beach.

Anger
Anger is like a fierce, exploding volcano.
It tastes like rotten Brussels sprouts.
It smells like a burning fire.
It looks like a dark and gloomy tunnel that never seems to end.
It sounds like thunder booming in the sky.
It feels like being torn to shreds.

Chloe Rogers (9)
Valley Gardens Middle School

Emotions

Happiness is pink like candyfloss.
It smells like the sweet scent of flowers.
It tastes like strawberry milkshake.
It sounds like laughter.
It feels like a soft cuddly teddy.
It looks like a hot sunny day.

Anger is red like a demon's eye.
It sounds like a volcano erupting.
It smells like an old damp sewer.
It tastes like cold rice pudding.
It looks like a charging bull.
It feels like a horrible nightmare.

Lydia Ruddick (9)
Valley Gardens Middle School

Anger

If anger was a colour,
I would choose red,
Like the thorn of a rose.

If anger was a sound,
I would choose *grrrr,*
Like an angry teacher.

If you could taste anger,
I would choose it to be sour,
Like the sour Starbursts.

If you could smell anger,
I would choose soot,
Like from a dirty chimney.

If you could see anger,
I would choose a devil,
Like from the depths of Hell.

If you could feel anger,
I would choose it to be rough,
Just like tarmac.

Joe Foreman (9)
Valley Gardens Middle School

Christmas

C elebrating the birth of Jesus
H appy faces on this day
R eindeer prancing by your window
I cicles hanging from rooftops
S anta climbing down the chimney
T insel hanging on the tree
M istletoe, for lots of kisses
A ngels singing Christmas carols
S nowflakes fluttering in the sky.

Jolene McIntyre (9)
Valley Gardens Middle School

Ten Punky Pop Stars

10 punky pop stars
Drinking bottles of wine
One snapped a nail
And then there were 9

9 punky pop stars
Trying to look great
One got quite spotty
And then there were 8

8 punky pop stars
Happy they're not in Heaven
One slipped and bashed their head
And then there were 7

7 punky pop stars
Trying to move some bricks
One dropped one on her toe
And then there were 6

6 punky pop stars
Surprised to be alive
One was not good at solos
And then there were 5

5 punky pop stars
Going to go and explore
One got captured
And then there were 4

4 punky pop stars
Keeping a monkey
One got itchy fleas
And then there were 3

3 punky pop stars
Hanging round the loo
One missed the coach
And then there were 2

2 punky pop stars
Having lots of fun
One ran away
And then there was 1

1 punky pop star
Thinking the day is done
Fell asleep on the swing
And then there were none!

Jenny Mills (9)
Valley Gardens Middle School

Love And Hate

Love
Love is like sitting on a cloud.
It tastes like sweet sugar.
It smells like red roses.
It looks like a soft pink heart.
It sounds like a gentle breeze.
It feels like I'm happy with my family.

Love is like having fun.
It tastes like rosy apples.
It smells like floating blossom.
It looks like a gentle flower.
It sounds like an empty swimming pool.
It feels like I'm with all my friends.

Hate
Hate is like being alone.
It smells like grey smoke.
It tastes like burnt toast.
It looks like a piece of black paper
It sounds like horrid loud thunder.
It feels like sitting in the rain.

Hate is like a freezing bath.
It smells like a rotten shoe.
It tastes like a cold Sunday dinner.
It looks like black storm clouds.
It sounds like my screaming sister.
It feels like sleeping in the snow.

Nina Dungworth (9)
Valley Gardens Middle School

Simile Poem

See my hair, it's as white as snow,
It shines in the dark - what a glow!

As blue as the ocean that's my eyes,
Looking up at those beautiful skies!

Elephants' ears are big, mine are too,
But you won't find me in a country park or zoo!

My nose like a tissue is soft and squidgy
I'm really glad it's not big and ridgy!

Like the winner of a tennis match my mouth has a smile
Sometimes it's sad but that's only once in a while!

Hands as big as shovels, that's what they are
As goalie on the football team they've been great so far!

With a body as strong as a powerful ox
I can punch my way out of a cardboard box!

My legs are as tanned
As the golden sand!

Last but not least there's my feet, but I wish
That they did not smell like an old smelly fish.

Daniel Simpson (9)
Valley Gardens Middle School

A Crocodile

Swims like a shark
Smiles like a rhino
Feet as big as children
As lazy as a pig
As vicious as a tiger
Like a tree sprouting through the ground
As long as a car
Like a vicious elephant
As hard as metal
Like a big wall of bricks.

Robert Ferry (9)
Valley Gardens Middle School

10 Fit Footballers

10 fit footballers standing in a line
One tripped up and then there were nine.

9 fit footballers standing at the gate
One missed the bus and then there were 8.

8 fit footballers going down to Devon
One forgot to go and then there were 7.

7 fit footballers playing pooh sticks
One fell in the water and then there were 6.

6 fit footballers practising a dive
One got hurt and then there were 5.

5 fit footballers standing at the door
One jammed his finger and then there were 4.

4 fit footballers climbing up a tree
One fell out and then there were 3

3 fit footballers wondering what to do
One got fed up and then there were 2.

2 fit footballers wondering where they'd gone
One went to look and then there was 1.

1 fit footballer when extra time had gone
Whistle blew, buses went, then there were none.

Sam Thompson (9)
Valley Gardens Middle School

A Poem About The World

The world is round,
Like a football that has been blasted into the sky.
If you follow the ground around the world,
A country you will find.
The seas and oceans crash their sound,
Watch them smash and spray.
Earth is where animals, humans and plants are found.
Take care and protect nature and the environment around.

William McPherson (9)
Valley Gardens Middle School

10 Wacky Scientists

10 wacky scientists
Experimenting on a mine
But everything went wrong
And then there were 9

9 wacky scientists
One was late
And when the boss found out
There were only 8

8 wacky scientists
One had arrived at eleven
And the others were doing bad chemistry
And then there were 7

7 wacky scientists
Throwing around sticks
When all of a sudden there was a bang!
And then there were 6

6 wacky scientists
Messing with a beehive
When all of a sudden there was a big buzzing sound
And then there were 5

5 wacky scientists
One fell on the floor
And said, 'Oow!'
And then there were 4

4 wacky scientists
One wanted to be free
But when he tried to escape
There were only 3

3 wacky scientists
One needed to go to the loo
But when he wet his pants
There were only 2

2 wacky scientists
One was playing in the sun
But when he tripped over
There was only 1

1 wacky scientist
Eating a hot bun
But when the lab closed
There were none.

Tom Scott (9)
Valley Gardens Middle School

Happiness To Loneliness

Happiness feels like freshly cut grass
On a hot summer's day.
Happiness tastes like a house of marshmallows
And sweets too.
Happiness sounds like two little robins
Peacefully singing in the sun.
Happiness reminds me of
All the times with my family.
Happiness sounds like violins
Playing in a grand hall.
Happiness smells like seaweed
Rolling around in the deep ocean.

Loneliness is like you're alone in an
Empty desert of your own.
Loneliness is black and red like
An angry vampire.
Loneliness sounds like technology,
Like the sewing machine.
Loneliness is really hard,
Like a dinosaur's scales.
Loneliness reminds me of lots of horrible
Deaths in the world.
Loneliness tastes like lots of sour lemons
Being squashed into your mouth.
Loneliness is as cold as the Arctic
In a winter blizzard.

Jamie Farnworth (9)
Valley Gardens Middle School

From Fear To Peace

Fear is white like a ghost
That comes round corridors to spook you.
Fear tastes like cold rice pudding
That has been on the table for days.
Fear feels like pain
That increases each moment.
Fear smells like burnt food
That you loved to eat until that day.
Fear sounds like a swirling hurricane
That demolishes and destroys everything in its path.

Peace is as colourful as the rainbow
That dazzles in the mind like glittering stars.
Peace tastes like cubes of chocolate
That melts in the mouth like the sun slowly setting.
Peace feels like heaven on Earth
That goes on forever.
Peace smells like freshly baked bread
That makes the mouth water just thinking about it.
Peace sounds like the twittering of birds
That gaily spread their wings and soar over every acre of land.

Rebecca McGarry (9)
Valley Gardens Middle School

Irish Dancing

Prancing, jumping, tapping fast.
Kicking, flicking, dancers pass.
Exhilarating, feels like flying; panting like a dog.
Feet stamping like an army troop;
It makes me dizzy like loop-the-loop
Hair with curls bounce up and down,
I'm surprised it doesn't make a sound.
Lily-white socks and jet-black feet,
Turned-out toes that look so neat.
When I go home and go to sleep
All I see is dancers' feet.

Jessica Ivison (9)
Valley Gardens Middle School

My Horse Poem

H orses can jump,
O thers can race,
R iders can't run at the very same pace,
S ome horses are pretty, some horses are ugly,
E verybody thinks they're still lovely!
S ome can gallop as fast as lightning.

A lso ponies are wonderful,
N o one should hate them,
D early I'd love one,

P onies are just as pretty,
O h how could you not have one?
N ice or nasty,
I still think they're great,
E njoy them if you have one,
S o if you have one you're lucky!

Sarah Glendinning (9)
Valley Gardens Middle School

Colourful Emotions

Anger is red-hot like fire.
Anger is red like a boiling pool of lava.
Anger is red-hot like a burning fire.
Anger is red like blood.

Excitement is bright yellow like sand.
Excitement is yellow like a nice hot day.
Excitement is yellow like going crazy.
Excitement is yellow like the sun.

Sadness is a depressing blue like the sea.
Sadness is blue like a dripping tear.
Sadness is blue like having a sad feeling.
Sadness is blue like being unhappy.

David Wilson (9)
Valley Gardens Middle School

Fireworks

Whoosh, it flies with burning power,
Bang! Exploding like a dazzling flower,
Coloured stars fill the sky,
Until they fade away and die.

A loud booming fills the air,
Coming from a gigantic flare,
Lots of fireworks in the night,
Filling up the sky with light.

Beautiful colours before my eyes,
My ears are filled with cheers and sighs.

The smell of smoke is all around,
Bonfires making a crackling sound.

I love fireworks, but beware!
You always need to take great care.
If you do you'll be alright,
And enjoy your Bonfire Night.

Sean Findlay (10)
Valley Gardens Middle School

Emotion

Anger is red like a piece of fire
Anger is blue like a steaming pool
Anger is purple like someone furious
Anger is yellow like a steaming desert

Excitement is yellow like the sun
Excitement is blue like a pool
Excitement is orange like a basketball
Excitement is blue like a football

Evil is dark red like a volcano
Evil is red like blood
Evil is blue like someone drowning in water
Evil is red like a boy falling out of a tree.

Joseph Robson (9)
Valley Gardens Middle School

My Strange House

Mischievous bees in the drawers
Alligator in the corridor
Upside down, turn around
In my crazy house

With an elephant in the bath
A mad monkey in the sink
Upside down, limp around
In my mad house

In the haunted lounge
I saw a bold brown cow
Oh no hop around
In the silly house

In my roller skates was a dog
And on my chair was a reading horse
Upside down, run around
In my nugget house

I need a method
I won't receive a punch
Upside down, monkey around
In my cracked house

I set up the dynamite
Then there goes a *boom*
Like a crane in my house
My shimmered house that is a pile of rice.

Scott Rutherford (10)
Valley Gardens Middle School

Space

Space is like a huge planet that holds all the rest.
The sun in the middle.
It is filled with unseen worlds.
Meteorites crashing and bashing about in deep space.
The sun like a fire that never burnt out . . .

Luke Beattie (9)
Valley Gardens Middle School

Hallowe'en

Spooky ghosts wander through the streets,
Giving people sudden frights,
Searching for lollies and sweets,
Lurking in the dark night.

Witches with their brooms,
Vampires with their fangs,
Fireworks making booms,
And fireworks making bangs.

There are no more lights,
There are no more shouts,
There are no more frights,
And the pumpkin's gone out.

Adam Shorthouse (9)
Valley Gardens Middle School

The Hawk

The hawk is a strict beast,
In its cage like a tree.
Its tree is its hideout.

It flies around the whole city.
And picks off your hat from your
Headless head, so you wouldn't
Want to find one up above you.

The hawk's eyes are fire,
Fearsome falcon, burning, blazing
Eyes like a bonfire burning up
The wood and fireworks shooting
Into the midnight sky with the beast
Flying over.

Courtney Ward (9)
Valley Gardens Middle School

Winter

Winter has . . .
The soft scrunching snow,
Trees are bare without their
Jacket of leaves.
Winter has . . .
Christmas trees, a prickly bush,
New year when everybody is
Happy.
Winter has . . .
Sledging children flying down
Hills like prancing deer,
Christmas cards, well, is
There one for me?

Edward Thompson (9)
Valley Gardens Middle School

Christmas

The robin sat
On a Christmas
Tree chirping happily

Snow falling gently
On the hard rock pavement

Santa Claus sitting on his
Sledge whistling 'Merry Christmas'

Rudolph flying through the air
And his nose as red as a tomato

Christmas lights sparkling in the air,
All different colours like twinkling stars
Everywhere around you.

Max Emery (9)
Valley Gardens Middle School

Loopy Emotions

Boredom feels like a never-ending death
In the darkness of the night.
Boredom smells like a mouldy piece of bread
Left and forgotten out in the sun.
Boredom's colour is like a stormy night
Black and grey and very, very dull.
Boredom tastes like a cup of sea water
Left in a cupboard all year long, dry and sandy.
Boredom looks like the Devil
In a red and fiery place.

Excitement tastes like a dream
Come true.
Excitement sounds like a lullaby
Of the angel on a summer's day.
Excitement's colour is like the colours of the rainbow
In your back garden.
Excitement feels like a fire cracker
Going off in your tummy.
Excitement looks like a lava lamp
Bright and bubbly, sitting in the sun.

Thomas Sherreard (9)
Valley Gardens Middle School

Pain

Pain is the colour black,
It smells of blood,
It feels like a deep, dark hole in your heart,
It tastes of stale bread.
You try to run away from it but it keeps pulling you back,
You can't see it but it's there,
You can't hear it for it does not make a sound.
Scary shivering screams,
The hairs on your back stand on end.
You try to scream but nothing comes out of your mouth,
No matter what, everyone is scared of pain!

Bethany Wilson (9)
Valley Gardens Middle School

Mixed Emotions

Love is pink like a beautiful rose
Blossoming in the spring.
Love feels like a butterfly inside you
Flying around your heart.
Love looks like a tropical bird
Watching her eggs hatch.
Love sounds like an angel singing
Sitting upon a fluffy cloud.
Love smells like sweet-smelling lavender
Growing in the fields.

Hate is black like the dark pupil of an eye
Staring at you fiercely from across the room.
Hate feels like you're inside an oven
Getting hotter and hotter until you burn.
Hate looks like a dark alley
Infested with rats that are going to poison you.
Hate sounds like an old organ
Playing loudly at a funeral.
Hate smells like bitter lemon
Going down your throat, making you sick.

Sofia Birch (9)
Valley Gardens Middle School

Bonfire Night

Fireworks whizzing, banging, pop,
Brightening the night sky to light.
Catherine wheels spinning dizzily,
Like a whirlpool drawing my attention.

Crackling showers of shimmering sparks,
Affecting the moonlit sky.
The smell of gunpowder travelling in clouds,
Is the smell of my Bonfire Night.

Joshua Gribbin (9)
Valley Gardens Middle School

Feet

My old nana has terrible feet
From walking and hobbling down the street
They've been squeezed into high heels, slipped into wellies
And squashed into slippers ever so smelly.

My little sister has beautiful feet
And also her ten toes are ever so sweet
They've been growing and growing,
Needing more shoes and new shoes
How many more can she choose?

My active feet are ever so small
That's quite surprising 'cause I'm so tall
We've been looking for trainers everywhere
But can't agree on an Adidas pair.

Lucy Sherburn (9)
Valley Gardens Middle School

Emotions

Being upset is dark blue like a roaring ocean,
Being upset is sky-blue like a flowing river.

Being excited is yellow like the steaming sun,
Being excited is multicoloured like a rainbow.

Anger is red like an erupting volcano,
Anger is black like an exploding mountain.

Happiness is purple like party balloons,
Happiness is orange like fresh spring flowers.

Jealousy is green like slimy, sloppy toads,
Jealousy is pink like a sunburnt polar bear.

Being pleasant is orange like fresh fruit,
Being pleasant is purple like a summer's day.

Aoife Oliver (9)
Valley Gardens Middle School

Toyland

I run into my room
Look at my toys
They fill me with joy
My soldiers made out of plastic
Absolutely fantastic
The Xbox Generation
Let's have a celebration.

A soft cuddly bear, round and bright
Lots of other toys in my sight
My computer screen springs into action
I need to close my blind just a fraction
My mum shouts, 'Time for tea'
Roast chicken, my favourite for me.

Jamie Chenylle-Proctor (9)
Valley Gardens Middle School

Dogs

Big ones, small ones,
Fat and thin ones,
None of them are my type,
Chocolate-brown and creamy white,
Nearly but not quite,
My type of dog would be, I think,
Maybe a she that's chocolate-brown,
With big soft paws and beady brown eyes,
But wait, that's my dog,
So big ones, small ones,
Fat and thin ones,
Forget all of them,
Because I have the best dog in the world.

Jamie Leighton (9)
Valley Gardens Middle School

Clara

Clara, Clara is so white,
Sleeps in the day,
Hunts at night

Clara, Clara is so white
Big strong jaws,
Sharp long claws

Clara, Clara is so white
Tickle her,
She might bite

Clara, Clara is so white
Eats mice,
How nice!

Clara, Clara is so white
Defends the garden
Loves to fight

Clara, Clara is so white
Like a lion
Loves to bite

Clara, Clara is so white,
Cuddly, curly, cute and bright

Clara, Clara, who is she?
Give you a clue . . .
She can climb a tree
Sometimes happy
Sometimes sad
Sometimes lazy
Sometimes mad

Clara, Clara, is my pet cat
Miaow, miaow
Now that is that!

Luke Stronach (9)
Valley Gardens Middle School

What Emotions Are

Anger is red like a burning comet
That speeds so fast through space,
Leaving destruction behind.

Anger feels like a raging inferno
Swallowing anything in its path,
And burning down everything else.

Anger feels violent like a wild animal
Charging at something else,
And enjoying all the pain.

Anger is like molten lava
Seeping down the mountain,
Almost excited, yet horrid.

Anger sounds like millions of bulls
Storming through a village,
Causing despair and sadness.

Anger smells like smoke
Snaking up your nose,
And deciding to crush your brain.

Tolerance is warm like a morning breeze
That cools everyone down,
Eliminating all anger.

Tolerance tastes like a chocolate pudding
Coated and warm . . . yum,
The perfect thing you could eat.

Tolerance sounds like several happy rabbits
Hopping through a field full of fruit,
Without a care in the world.

Tolerance is white like a peaceful cloud
Floating through the air so slow,
That makes people happy.

Johnny Cattell (10)
Valley Gardens Middle School

Growing Up

One second old
I'm out my mummy's tummy
Gazing gratefully at my new world
Staring serenely at my mummy
Cuddling me like a soft teddy bear.

Now I'm wearing silky dresses
Trousers, tops and shiny shoes
I'm playing with dolls
Bouncing on my trampoline
Like a nine-year-old would do.

Now I'm into fashion
Boys and make-up too
Shopping and stropping
Are my favourite things
They are what I love to do.

Now I go to work each day
And earn myself a living
Life is busy
With a house to keep
I'm stressed, but having fun.

I'm gazing gratefully at my new world
As a very happy mum
My new baby is cuddled in
Ready to start its journey
In the big wide world.

Emily Wright (9)
Valley Gardens Middle School

Happiness

Happiness is pink like a flamingo in the water.
Happiness is like stars sparkling in the sky.
Happiness looks like horses playing in a field.
Happiness smells like chips in a pan.
Happiness tastes like candyfloss.

Madeleine Ord (9)
Valley Gardens Middle School

Summer

Summer is gold like the gleaming sun,
Hearing laughter of children having fun.

Children not wanting the day to end,
In the morning it starts all over again.

And the flowers opening for summer,
Thirsting for water and bursting with colour.

Birds singing in the slight cool breeze,
As they sit on their trees.

Children always wanting ice creams,
While they sit next to the sparkling stream.

Beth Ramsay (9)
Valley Gardens Middle School

Summer

Summer is gold like the glistening sun.
And summer smells like a freshly baked bun.
Summer tastes like chocolate melting in your mouth.
It's the tastiest chocolate in the south.
Summer tastes like freshly baked bread.
Summer looks like injured footballers lying in bed.

Robbie Potter (9)
Valley Gardens Middle School

Summer

Summer is gold like the gleaming sun.
Hear the screaming children having fun.
Fresh, hot toffee apples sitting there steaming.
Smell the cotton candy, nice and sticky.
Look at the funfair lit up in the bright night sky.
Sand slipping out of your hand.
Last year's summer going abroad to see my Auntie Ward.

Daniel McIntyre (9)
Valley Gardens Middle School

Spain

I like to go to a hot place called Spain.
To get there I need to take a roaring plane.
Spain is as magical as the golden sun.
It's like listening to children having fun.
Spain is as hot as a burning match.
It's as glorious as a football match.
In Spain I went to a creepy house.
In the night I saw a mouse.

Aidan Walker (9)
Valley Gardens Middle School

I Walk Down A Path

I walk down a path
As autumn begins,
Crunch, crack beneath my feet
Looking down I see crimson, yellow and red.
Trees stripped bare as if getting ready to take a bath.
Twigs snapping, falling down amongst the leaves.
Autumn is here.

Kristopher Nef (9)
Valley Gardens Middle School

The Winter

Winter is white as the ice-cold snow.
The snow feels like a velvet coat.
It's as cold as a fridge.
You can hear people having fun.
The snow on my lips is like melting ice cream.
The snow looks like icing on a cake.
White as far as I can see.
Crunch, crunch, crunch, under my boots
Like biting a cornet,
And I feel happy as I smile.

Ella Reveley (9)
Valley Gardens Middle School

Best To Worst

Excitement is orange like the sun
Beating down on you intensely.
Excitement looks like a graceful unicorn
Galloping in a dreamland.
Excitement smells like a chocolate pancake
About to enter your mouth.
Excitement tastes like strawberries and chocolate
Falling into a bowl of ice cream.
Excitement feels like a wild tiger
Giving you a piggyback in a jungle.
Excitement sounds like a bird
Singing on a tree with its mate.

Boredom is black like the longest night
Moonless and dusky.
Boredom looks like a paralysed fox
Alone in the middle of the wood.
Boredom smells like a trash can
Halfway full with rotten food and broken ornaments.
Boredom tastes like worms
Slithering all the way down your throat.
Boredom smells like a warthog
Singing in a smelly swamp all alone.

Dominic Widdas (10)
Valley Gardens Middle School

Winter

Snow here, snow there,
Snow everywhere,
Hear children laughing in the street,
Getting wet and cold feet.
Yearning for Christmas to come,
And mouths watering for that tasty cake.
Snow falling from the sky.
Are you ready for Christmas pie?

Madeline Duggan (9)
Valley Gardens Middle School

All Good Things Come To An End

Happiness is like after a gloomy day a rainbow appears.
Happiness feels like you have just won £100 grand in the lottery.
Happiness is red like the sunset on a summer's evening.
Happiness smells like lavender growing on a summer's day
Hand-picked by professionals.
Happiness sounds like birds tweeting up in the fresh-smelling trees.
Happiness is like a shimmer of light showing you out of a
Pitch-black cave.

Sadness is like going downstairs on Christmas Day
And there being no presents.
Sadness is like a big, dull, empty wasteland
That has just been burned.
Sadness tastes like a cold and bitter lemon
That makes your taste buds feel sick.
Sadness is like a gunshot off in the distance striking someone down.
Sadness smells like fresh-cut onions picked on a winter's day
Sadness is like having ten lots of homework in one day.

Thomas Wheeler (9)
Valley Gardens Middle School

Anger And Happiness

Anger is red like lava
Anger is black like the sign of death
Anger is grey like a twister.
Anger is brown like a brown Smartie.

Happiness is orange like an orange.
Happiness is yellow like SpongeBob SquarePants.
Happiness is blue like the sea

Excitement is blue like going to the swimming pool.
Excitement is green like going to a football match.

Happiness is brown like bacon.
Happiness is white like cold snow.
Happiness is gold like opening my Christmas presents.

Jack Cochrane (9)
Valley Gardens Middle School

Twisted Emotions

Happiness is like gentle butterflies
Fluttering by on a gorgeous summer's day.
Happiness tastes like fluffy candyfloss
Fizzing in your mouth.
Happiness is like the colour of a
Rosy, pale pink petal.
Happiness is like a fairground ride
Filling you with excitement.
Happiness smells like cakes in the oven
Ready to be iced.

Sadness is like everything turning black or white
With rain pouring down.
Sadness sounds like horrible organs
Playing at a funeral.
Sadness tastes like mouldy apples
Rotting in the bin.
Sadness is the colour of grey,
Boring and plain.
Sadness feels as if the world has ended,
And is never coming back again.

Jennifer Guillan (10)
Valley Gardens Middle School

Frustration Turns To Contentment

Frustration is like a volcano bubbling inside your brain.
Frustration looks like a rainy day when there is nothing to do.
Frustration is red like lava burning up inside you.
Frustration smells like your worst meal cooking in the oven.

Contentment looks like a baby sleeping quietly in a cot.
Contentment smells like your favourite meal cooking in the oven.
Contentment is pink like hearts floating in the sky.

Callum Lake (9)
Valley Gardens Middle School

Different Emotions

Jealousy is blistering cold snow,
Falling in the night.
Jealousy is a cloud
Floating overhead.
Jealousy is a plane
Landing in the airport.
Jealousy is darkness,
Filling the sky with hope.
Jealousy is a storm
Growing wilder every minute.
Jealousy is the blue sky above us,
Lighting up the ground.

Trust is the bright sun
Shining in the sky.
Trust is newly laid grass
Growing in the sunlight.
Trust is the solution of a problem
At the end of a hard journey.
Trust is a safe home
Waiting to welcome company.
Trust is a mouth-watering sweet
Waiting to be eaten.
Trust is endless trouble
Cut in half.
Trust is a polished floor
Easy to walk on.
Trust is the sound of voices
Calling trouble to stop.

James Bradford (10)
Valley Gardens Middle School

Switching Emotions

Boredom sounds like a bell,
Chiming midnight.
Boredom smells like the fumes of a car,
Like on a rainy day
Boredom is grey like a foggy day.
Boredom tastes like a slice of bread,
Old, stale and hard
Boredom is like an angry child
Grounded in the holidays.
Boredom is like drinking a sleeping potion
And getting sleepier every second.
Boredom is like being alone,
In the cold, dark woods.

Excitement tastes like spicy food,
Fizzing up your tongue.
Excitement is like Tony Blair
Waiting for the election results to come in.
Excitement is like bubbles,
Bubbling from a pot.
Excitement smells like a rose garden
Blooming in the summer.
Excitement is like a rabbit
Hopping from danger.
Excitement is like a shaken-up Coke can
Ready to shower you with spray.
Excitement is like the memory of a holiday
On a fast roller coaster.
Excitement sounds like the dance music
At a funky disco.

Sally Earl (9)
Valley Gardens Middle School

Twisted Emotions

Love feels like a light feather
Falling gently out of a big fluffy cloud.
Love is the pink of your heart
When you fall deeply in love.
Love tastes like candyfloss and ice cream
At a summer fair.
Love reminds me of being cared for
At Christmas by my family.
Love looks like two doves flying
In peace in Heaven.
Love sounds like a harp
Playing at a wedding.
Love smells like beautiful red and yellow rose petals
Falling gently in the winter.

Hatred feels like a cold snowflake
Falling down the back of your T-shirt.
Hatred is like the red of blood
Bleeding out and confusing your brain.
Hatred tastes like hot chilli peppers
On fire in your mouth.
Hatred smells like the burning wood
On Bonfire Night.
Hatred looks like a bull racing
At a harmless person in an arena.
Hatred sounds like a pack of wolves
Attacking their prey.
Hatred is like the memory
Of falling out with my friends and being all alone.

Hannah Redhead (10)
Valley Gardens Middle School

Fear And Bravery

Bravery is like a warm yellow blanket
When the sun is rising.
Bravery is like a crowd of people
Congratulating you.
Bravery is like a shiny medal
Wrapped around your neck.
Bravery is like a memory that's magical
Is blowing in the wind of change!
Bravery tastes like lemon bon-bons
Melting on your tongue.
Bravery is like your favourite dream
Dancing in the moonlight.
Bravery is like your best friend
Welcoming you back home.

Fear is like the ghost of shame
Haunting you for life.
Fear is like an unhealthy green
Similar to eaten grass.
Fear is like a little hurricane
Pushing you towards the end.
Fear is like a group of cavemen
Hammering your brain.
Fear is like a sour lime
Bursting the bubbles on your tongue.
Fear is a smell as weird as
Beetroot tickling your tummy.
Fear is like a voice nagging you,
Whilst leading you to Hell.
Fear is like a dagger
Killing your bravery.

Victoria Tong (10)
Valley Gardens Middle School

Sadness Turns To Happiness

Sadness tastes like the salty sea
Bubbling in your mouth.
Sadness is like a dark and gloomy cellar
With homework creeping up on you.
Sadness smells like fresh onions
Watering your eyes.
Sadness feels like an icy shiver up your spine
Which drowns all the happiness from your heart.
Sadness is black like the winter midnight sky
Cold, dull and gloomy.
Sadness looks like spooky coffins
It makes your heart miss a beat.

Happiness looks like yellow daffodils
Which are like stars around your heart.
Happiness smells like fresh coconuts from Africa
Making your mind relax.
Happiness feels warm like a fire that is heating,
Warming up your body.
Happiness sounds like birds tweeting
Welcoming you to a new day.
Happiness tastes like marshmallows melting in hot chocolate
Making your body twinkle.
Happiness is yellow like a midday sun
Which makes you feel sleepy.

Aine Singleton (9)
Valley Gardens Middle School

Your Eyes

Your eyes are as brown as mud.
Your eyes are as blue as the sky.
Your eyes are as green as grass.
Your eyes are as brown as anything.
Your eyes are as blue as anything.
Your eyes are as green as anything.
Your eyes are eyes.

Scott Wraith (9)
Valley Gardens Middle School

Twisted Emotions

Love is as red as a rose,
Dancing in the sunlight.
Love is like gazing out from the harbour,
At the boats sailing by.
Love feels as warm as the summer breeze,
When running through the blossom.
Love is as soft as feathers
Inside your pillow case.

Hatred is as grey as an evil rain cloud
Going to explode.
Hatred tastes like 100 lemons,
That have been dipped in vinegar.
Hatred looks like a volcano,
About to erupt and destroy all the land.
Hatred feels like hard rock,
Being hit off your head.
Hatred feels like screaming as loud as you can,
So everything smashes into a million pieces.

Lucy Olson (9)
Valley Gardens Middle School

My Poem

The sea is near us but when we are near it
Times are better for everything that can see it.

The sun is now setting but in the morning it will arise
Big, beautiful and also wise.

The nature of Earth is in our hands
So we should keep it on its land
But we should be fair and lend a helping hand.

Our friends and family need us to stay
And lend a hand all the way,
We should be kind and helpful too
And that means everyone will be kind to you.

Lorena Weepers (9)
Valley Gardens Middle School

10 Huge Daleks

10 huge Daleks
Standing in a line
One shot another
Then there were 9

9 huge Daleks
Standing in a line
One tried to kill a bird
Then there were 8

8 huge Daleks
Lurking round the TARDIS
One flew it to Heaven
Then there were 7

7 huge Daleks
Invading Devon
One crashed into sticks
Then there were 6

6 huge Daleks
Standing ready for battle
One did a dive
Then there were 5

5 huge Daleks
Standing in a hive
One got stuck in the door
Then there were 4

4 huge Daleks
Standing in a tree
One fell out
Then there were 3

3 huge Daleks
Lurking in the loo
One went to the zoo
Then there were 2.

2 huge Daleks
Thinking they were done
One ran off
Then there was 1

1 huge Dalek
Standing on his own
Fell into a lake
Then there were none!

Mark Blyth (9)
Valley Gardens Middle School

Mixed Emotions

Jealousy is a hissing snake
With venom like the sting of an angry bee.
Jealousy is cold hard steel
As plain as plain can be.
Jealousy is a howling cat
With eyes as bright as diamonds.
Jealousy is putrid green
Like the Emerald City of Oz.
Jealousy is a giant lemon
That tastes sourer than the salty sea.
Jealousy is choking smoke
Erupting from a vat of poison.

Love is a soft pink rose
With dewdrops sparkling in the light.
Love is smooth, smooth silk
Rippling and shimmering gently.
Love is heavenly cupids
And lovebirds and doves singing sweetly.
Love is a small light cloud
As drifting and soft as can be.
Love is sweet, sickly honey
Its sugary aroma overwhelming.
Love is a big soft peach
Slowly spreading its juice around your mouth.

Laura Milburn (9)
Valley Gardens Middle School

Happiness Turns To Sadness

Happiness is like a woolly sheep
Galloping around a field
Happiness is yellow like the bright sun
Shining down on you.
Happiness is like a content dove
Flying over the hills.
Happiness is like a chocolate cake
Smelling so deliciously fine.
Happiness is like a fluffy polar bear
Digging in the snow.
Happiness is like a trickling stream
Flowing to a river.
Happiness is like a sunny buttercup
Swaying in the breeze.

Sadness is like a barren desert
With nobody there except you.
Sadness is like an abandoned puppy
Feeling ignored and neglected.
Sadness is like an empty graveyard
With sorrow flooding to your eyes.
Sadness is like a dull dark cloud
Just waiting to rain on you.
Sadness is like a sour lemon
Making you want to squirm.
Sadness is like someone dying
Making you want to cry.
Sadness is like a crumpled piece of paper
Getting thrown in the bin.

Louise Russell (9)
Valley Gardens Middle School

Rage Turns To Peace

Rage is like angry shots of thunder and lightning
Rumbling in your tummy like a firework.
Rage is red like a volcano
Erupting fiercely.
Rage is like a burnt meal
That burns your tongue like chopped-up chillies.
Rage is like a cooker
Burning your finger.
Rage is like a lion
Catching its prey.
Rage is like a cigarette
Burning in an ashtray.
Rage is like a knot
Wrapped around your angry heart.
Rage is like a dog
Killing a cat.

Peace is like a warm sun,
Heating you up on a winter's day.
Peace is like a woolly jumper
Been knitted just for you.
Peace is pink like a girl's bedroom.
Peace is like a soft cuddly teddy bear.
Peace is like relaxing
In bed all day.
Peace is like a polar bear
Raising its cubs.
Peace is like a cloud
Coming towards you to take you to Heaven.
Peace is like a happy moment
Happening again.

Cameron Barlow (9)
Valley Gardens Middle School

Sorrow And Joy

Sorrow is dark like a raging rain cloud
Ready for a downfall.
Sorrow is as sharp as nails
Digging into your skin.
Sorrow smells like gas
Circling around your body.
Sorrow is like a never-ending silence
That never goes away.
Sorrow is as if you are frozen inside a block of ice
And you cannot escape.
Sorrow is like a pitch-black night
In the middle of winter.
Sorrow feels like a sharp arrowhead
Piercing your heart.
Sorrow is like a colourless rainbow
Without a pot of gold at the end.

Joy is like a warm, sunny day
Full of laughter, in the middle of summer.
Joy is like little children playing in the park
Underneath the blazing eyes of the sun.

Liam Gunning (9)
Valley Gardens Middle School

The Glitter Shaker

The eye twinkler
The sky brightener
The quiet crusher
The crackle smoker
The danger starter
The fire lighter
The child scarer
The colour whizzer
The whoosh banger
The glitter shaker.

Katherine Bradley (9)
Valley Gardens Middle School

Love Never Lasts

Love is like wedding bells
Ringing all day as if they will never stop.
Love is like a red valentine heart
Beating so fast.
Love is like a beautiful pink rose
Just opening on a hot summer's day.
Love is like the heavens have opened up
And will never close.
Love is like a harp
Playing a sweet and very soft tune.
Love is a dream come true.

Hatred sounds like a roaring lion
Trying to escape its hunter.
Hatred is black like a raging bull
Seeking his prey.
Hatred sounds like a herd of elephants
Running from a zoo.
Hatred smells like a burning flame
Melting your soul.

Adrienne Lake (9)
Valley Gardens Middle School

Emotions

Anger is as black as ash from a fire
Anger is red like a sizzling fire
Anger is deep black like a tall twister.

Unhappy is grey like a steaming kettle
Unhappy is dark blue like crashing waves
Unhappy is grey like stream from a train.

Happy is bright blue like the sky
Happy is light yellow like the beaming sun
Happy is silk-white like snow
Happy is the school holidays.

Matthew Robson (9)
Valley Gardens Middle School

The Colours Of Emotion

Anger is black like the night sky
Anger is red like blood
Anger is red like a burning fire

Excitement is yellow like the sparkling sun
Excitement is light blue like the daytime sky
Excitement is multicoloured like a rainbow

Depression is black like coal
Depression is red like an erupting volcano
Depression is red like tomato sauce

Happiness is yellow like pepper
Happiness is light blue like a blueberry
Happiness is light green like grapes

Sadness is black like a blackberry
Sadness is grey like an old man's hair
Sadness is grey like a donkey.

Andrew Bassett (9)
Valley Gardens Middle School

All Signs Of Autumn

Fireworks shooting up into the air, *whoosh, bang, bang.*
Pink, green, red, purple sparkling in the sky
Higher and higher up they go.

Trick or treaters knock, knock, knock,
Witches, devils, skeletons roam the streets
Broomsticks, bats, hats and cats,
Spiders, cobwebs, ghosts and painted faces or scary masks,
On the spooky Hallowe'en night.

Leaves collapsing to the ground,
Orange, scarlet and yellow
Footsteps scrunching on the ground.
Fog drifting in like a big hazy cloud.

All signs of autumn.

Jenny Ross (9)
Valley Gardens Middle School

All Bad Things Come To An End

Frustration is as violent as
The Undertaker cooking you to death
The blood bubbling and boiling through your head
It's increasing every minute.
Frustration is as loud as a pneumatic drill
Drilling through your heart.
Frustration is like you're locked in a fridge
And cold is going through your body
Your legs are frozen, your brain is dead.
Frustration is like Newcastle losing 9-0
And happening all the time.

Happiness is as calm as the Hawaiian sea
Floating through your body.
The boiling, bubbly water is going through your legs.
Happiness is like Cadbury's chocolate
Floating through your mouth every time you breathe.
Happiness is as good as white trainers
Glimmering in the moonlight, shining like the stars.
Happiness is like Newcastle winning the Champions League
And beating Sunderland in the final.

Callum Preston (9)
Valley Gardens Middle School

Coloured Emotions

Anger is blood-red like red-hot fire
Anger is sour red like a spinning tornado
Anger is bright red like jumping into boiling lava.

Sadness is dark black like the night sky
Sadness is light blue like a tear in your eye
Sadness is cold blue like frozen winter

Excitement is multicoloured like a cheerful party
Excitement is bright yellow like the bright sun
Excitement is light orange like a hot summer's day.

Charlotte Barron (10)
Valley Gardens Middle School

Love Turns To Hatred

Love is happy like a special childhood
When you're having a trip down memory lane.
Love smells like pink rose petals,
Daintily falling from the sky.
Love feels like a fluffy cloud
Floating up and down.
Love looks like the sparkling stars
That come out late at night.
Love makes you feel as happy as a newly married couple
On their honeymoon.
Love tastes like melted chocolate
Smooth and creamy in your mouth.
Love makes you feel as if you can reach the moon
Floating there in the Milky Way.

Hatred feels as cold as ice
Making you shiver and shake.
Hatred tastes as sour as a lemon
Making your mouth fizz.
Hatred smells as horrible as rotten eggs
Bunging up your nose.
Hatred is as hot as a boiling volcano
Bubbling inside your brain.
Hatred makes your heart feel twisted
When you are boiled with rage.
Hatred looks like a hole in the world
Dragging you inside.
Hatred looks like a strong hurricane
Destroying you inside.

Amy Bain (9)
Valley Gardens Middle School

Contentment Never Lasts

Contentment is like lying on a comfy bed,
Sleeping peacefully.
Contentment smells like clear air
Rushing through a forest.
Contentment feels like sitting in a forest
While wildlife runs free.
Contentment looks like an innocent squirrel
Hiding in a tree.
Contentment is green like the fresh forest grass
That's just been cut.
Contentment sounds like gerbils
Squeaking in a forest.
Contentment is like feeding ducks
While they swim for food.
Contentment sounds like a dog
Running and barking in peace.

Frustration is black like a dark cauldron
That bubbles with hot flames
Frustration smells like heated-up metal
Fresh from the kiln.
Frustration feels like lightning
Falling on your head.
Frustration sounds like gunshots
Being fired everywhere.
Frustration looks like an angry man
Shouting as loud as he can.
Frustration feels like wanting to punch someone
As hard as you can.
Frustration is like a dark cloud
Arriving above your head.

Ross Murray (9)
Valley Gardens Middle School

Feelings Of The Heart

Loneliness feels like you're burnt into ashes.
And don't exist.
Loneliness is like a dream
Where you wish you could close your eyes
And everything would be OK.
Loneliness tastes like a million trucks of lemons
Being shoved in your mouth.
Loneliness feels like you're only friends are the stars
And you are one part of the moon.
Loneliness smells like deadly, toxic gas.
Suffocating you down to the bloody waters of Earth's end.

Love is like a magic trick,
Where all your misery vanishes off the face of the Earth.
Love is like a newborn puppy,
Pouncing on top of you with glee.
Love feels like little angels are flying around your heart,
They have come down from Heaven with a golden bow
An arrow to bless your soul.
Love smells like a thousand roses,
Coming together with all sweet things
To make one mind soothing mixture.
Love sounds like a harp,
Gently plucking its strings into a long, calm sound
That begins to delicately glide through the fresh air
Into your ears.

Rachael Thornton (9)
Valley Gardens Middle School

The Time Of Autumn

Colourful leaves drifting gently to the frosted ground.
Red, crimson, russet, burgundy and brown.
Scarlet, peach, gold and silver.
These are the colours of the leaves falling from the withering trees.
Listen to the rumble of the tractors as the fields get ploughed.
Children planting spring bulbs.
Birds flying overhead, honking and crying, 'Winter is coming.'
Geese and swallows fly to warmer countries for the hard, cold winter.
Some animals staying behind to hibernate.
Hedgehogs, shrews, moles and mice.
Stock up on food before they hibernate.
You can hear the scurry, scurry, scurry
Of little feet in the bare hedges.
Animals gather materials to make snug warm beds.
'Boo,' Hallowe'en.
Everyone walking around in scary gruesome costumes.
Listen to all the children walking to and from houses saying,
'Trick or treat?'
Children carrying heavy bags full of tasty sweets.
Whoosh listen to the loud fireworks going off in all directions and the
Crackle, crackle of bright, hot bonfires.
Look at the Catherine wheels, rockets and fire crackers
Giving off so much light.
This is autumn.

Emily Davey (10)
Valley Gardens Middle School

Sky Shooter

Ear deafener
People amazer
Blue whizzer
Star chaser
Fire cracker
Night sparkler
Silence breaker
Colour maker
Light dancer
Neck acher
Spark creator
Crowd amuser
Smile producer
Time enjoyer
Conversation stopper.

Saoirse Stephenson-Lowe (9)
Valley Gardens Middle School

The Candy Man

In Mr Candy Man's shop
He sells bubbly fizzy pop
Marshmallows, fudge and
Chocolate
Gummi bears and minty rock.

Tubs of whirly liquorice
Stand upon his shelves
Jars of coloured bubblegums
While children help themselves.

In Mr Candy Man's shop
I like to spend my money
Especially on the nougat
That is covered in yummy
Honey.

Jedd Burrough (9)
Valley Gardens Middle School

Emotion Colours

Anger is red like the melted rock out of a volcano
Anger is black like an evil bat
Anger is red like the blood in a human
Anger is black like the sign of death

Happiness is as gold as the sun
Happiness is silver like the sparkling stars
Happiness is orange like the sunset
Happiness is green like the summer leaves

Sadness is light blue like the sky
Sadness is grey like the dull sky
Sadness is blue like the roaring sea
Sadness is black like the dark night

Joy is red like a balloon
Joy is white like the fluffy clouds
Joy is multicoloured like the rainbow
Joy is pink like candyfloss.

James Burt (9)
Valley Gardens Middle School

Emotions

Anger is boiling red like lava
Anger is black like the midnight hour
Anger is grey like the misty sky.

Happiness is yellow like the sun
Happiness is pink like a balloon
Happiness is blue like the sky.

Sadness is pale blue like the sea
Sadness is white like a cloud
Sadness is blue like a teardrop.

Excitement is orange like the spark from the sun.
Excitement is gold like lightning
Excitement is red like a planet.

Hannah Tompkins (9)
Valley Gardens Middle School

Colours Of Emotions

Anger is as red as lava from a volcano
Anger makes you explode like the first nuclear bomb
Anger is as black as a swirling black hole
Anger is as black as an open space in space.

Happiness is as yellow as the bright sun
Happiness is as light blue as the sky
Happiness is as yellow as SpongeBob Square Pants
Happiness is as light green as a leaf on a tree.

Illness is as grey as a dark cloud
Illness is as purple as a purple vein
Illness is as grey as my dad's hair
Illness is as purple as your face when you're holding your breath.

Excitement is as pink as my heart
Excitement is as multicoloured as a rainbow
Excitement is as orange as an orange
Excitement is as orange as an orange balloon.

Sadness is as blue as the deepest ocean
Sadness is as navy blue as my water bottle
Sadness is as blue as my old school's jumper
Sadness is as blue as the writing on a Valley Garden's jumper.

Bradley Smith (9)
Valley Gardens Middle School

Autumn Is Here

Leaves falling, dropping, tumbling softly down.
The wind blustery, breezy, blowing chilly.
The leaves coloured crimson, dark orange, light yellow, brown.
Celebrations of light bringing beautiful colours in the sky.
Thanksgiving, a massive feast.
Warm clothes, cosy woolly hats, jumpers, boots, thicker jackets.
Hibernation of the black bats, squirrels, spiky hedgehogs.
Autumn hangs in the air.

Lucy Richards (10)
Valley Gardens Middle School

Emotion Poem

Anger is black as coal from a burning fire
Anger is as red as lava from a volcano
Anger is as green as sprouts

Excited is as pink as a morning flower
Excited is as purple as a brand new carpet
Excited is as blue as the sea

Embarrassment is as pink as a rose
Embarrassment is as red as a red devil
Embarrassment is as purple as a plum

Happiness is as gold as treasure
Happiness is as brown as chocolate
Happiness is as yellow as a lemon.

Lucy Bruce (9)
Valley Gardens Middle School

Emotions

Anger is as red as a brand new brick.
Anger is as black as the night sky.
Anger is as grey as a cloud.
Anger is as orange as fire.

Happiness is as pink as some flowers.
Happiness is as yellow as the sun.
Happiness is as blue as the sky.

Depression is as blue as some tears.
Depression is as white as Heaven.
Depression is as green as the sea.
Depression is as purple as some balloons.

Sadness is as blue as a merit book.
Sadness is as golden as light.
Sadness is as green as a football pitch.
Sadness is as white as a glue stick.

Elliot Ross (9)
Valley Gardens Middle School

Happy And Sad Emotions Poem

Anger is blood-red like a spitting volcano.
Anger is black like a spell-binding eclipse.
Anger is red like a crackling fire.

Happiness is pink like a bunch of flowers.
Happiness is bright blue like the Australian coast.
Happiness is pink like a happy lion.

Illness is green like a mossy seat.
Illness is crimson like dripping blood.
Illness is green like alien slime.

Excitement is yellow like a whizzing roller coaster.
Excitement is blue like a Christmas present.
Excitement is yellow like thinking of a holiday.

Depression is dark blue like an empty cellar.
Depression is brown like a dirty hall.
Depression is dark blue like darkness.

Katherine Russell (9)
Valley Gardens Middle School

Emotions

Anger is bright like a burning fire
Anger is like steaming flames.
Anger is bright, blood-red like lava.

Happiness is light pink like a rose
Happiness is light yellow like the sun
Happiness is light yellow like a daisy

Sadness is like Brussels sprouts
Sadness is blue like the sky
Sadness is blue like water

Jealousy is green like vomit
Jealousy is green like grass
Jealousy is green like a frog.

Amy Fraser (9)
Valley Gardens Middle School

Celebrations Of Autumn

As the cold dark nights come quicker and quicker,
Children all excited knocking on the door for sweets,
Scary people in masks walking down the street,
Colourful costumes of witches and ghosts flying down,
Young people eating from their sacks.

Whoosh, bang fireworks dance.
Sparkling rockets go for miles, huge crashes.
Starry twisters making mixed lights.
Twinkle patterns,
Flashing, flying and floating around the black night sky,
Days get brighter as your average early spring day but not the temp.

Crops get harvest, gold sweetcorn,
Lots of juicy berries ready to pick.
Days are becoming winter, sadly autumn ends.
Fallen leaves are gone,
Most people come out,
And that is the end of autumn for another year.

Ailsa Ingham (9)
Valley Gardens Middle School

Emotion Poem

Anger is as red as a mean devil
Anger is as black as midnight.

Happiness is as gold as the bright sun
Happiness is as pink as roses.

Upsetting is as blue as the rain
Upsetting is as deep as the deepest ocean.

Excitement is as orangey as the sunset
Excitement is bright pink for a funfair.

Embarrassment is as red as a hot volcano
Embarrassment is as red as cherries.

Sarah Hamilton (9)
Valley Gardens Middle School

Autumn Signs

Leaves falling from cold icy trees,
Twisting, whirling through the sharp cold wind
All the bare trees are swaying swiftly back and forth.
No birds or animals in sight.
Everyone inside their warm cosy homes.
Crispy dead leaves, a range of different colours.
Scarlet, brown, yellow and gold.
Falling gently to the ground.
Birds have moved towards the sun
Some creatures hibernating underground
Nuts and berries for winter food
Fires flash on Bonfire Night.
Burning, crackling all over the dark sky.
Pumpkins, ghosts, skeletons.
Everywhere scary monsters
On spooky Hallowe'en night
Autumn is here.

Heather McQuade (9)
Valley Gardens Middle School

Emotions

Anger is black like a devil's eye
Anger is red like a stream of blood
Anger is purple like a dying flower
Anger is blue like a witch's dress

Happiness is pink like a pretty flower
Happiness is white like a wedding dress
Happiness is orange like a pair of skipping ropes
Happiness is yellow like a burning sun

Jealousy is green like Brussels sprouts
Jealousy is gold like a burning fire
Jealousy is brown like some horrid mould
Jealousy is silver like a bird's feather.

Kasha Korzonek (9)
Valley Gardens Middle School

The Oldies Vs The Backstreet Boys

Once there was a football team
Dazzling defenders, super strikers
Magnificent midfielders moved in a dream
And the goalies were fighters

The super-fit boys ran on to the pitch
Ready for the final battle
The next surprise hit them like a brick
They were against a team of grannies

These oldies played like Shearer
And tackled like raging bulls
The striker you had to fear her
As she loved having shots at the goal

5-0 was the score at the final whistle
The boys were like slow turtles
And felt like having a thistle
But the oldies were like tigers jumping over hurdles.

Liam Marriott (9)
Valley Gardens Middle School

Emotions Poem

Anger is red like a steaming volcano
Anger is black like coal
Anger is steaming grey like a splish, splosh rain cloud

Excitement is pink like seeing my cousins
Excitement is multicoloured like my birthday
Excitement is red like Christmas
Excitement is yellow like playing on my heelys
Nervous is grey like hearing bad news
Nervous is brown like flying on aeroplanes
Nervous is green like people hurting themselves
Nervous is purple like being in great danger

Sadness is blue like the deepest ocean.

Georgia Sturrock (10)
Valley Gardens Middle School

Zoo

One outrageous ostrich ordering omelettes on Sunday like an outlaw.
Two elegant elephants enjoying an endless entire pool,
As if they're in the Equator.
Three fierce, fast flaming flamingoes flinging flat, flying fried fruit,
Like a gang of fools.
Four hasty, horrible hogs hogging hungry helpful hedgehogs,
Like angry mad hatters,
Five domestic dangerous dingoes darting, digesting desperately,
Like constipated ducks.
Six sly, saucy snakes slip so slightly, and shouldn't shake sand,
Like a storm.
Seven rude, rusty, resting, rhinos, wrestling rocks,
Like they're rougher.
Eight limping, late, losing lions liked light lemon limes,
Like it was lovely to be a lion.
Nine naughty, nasty newts neatly nodded newly
Like there's something, something new every day.
Ten terrific koalas tasting tree leaves,
Like they lived only to eat that tree's leaves.

Josh Cogdon (9)
Valley Gardens Middle School

Emotions

Anger is red like a Nile monitor's tooth.
Anger is cramped like a photo booth.
Anger is sharp like a lion's claw.
Anger is loud like slamming a door.
Anger is fast like a striking snake,
It devours you like you would a cake.
Anger is deadly like a lionfish
That can poison you even if it's dead on a dish
Anger attacks you like a hammerhead shark,
Anger is rough like oak tree bark
And it is scary like a low maths mark.

Max Graham (10)
Valley Gardens Middle School

The Magic Adventures Of Rage And Tolerance

Rage is as red as a devil
Making a vicious curse on Hallowe'en.
Rage tastes like a spicy hot curry
Just coming out of the burning cooker.
Rage feels like a scorching chilli pepper
Boiling inside you.
Rage smells like bellows of smoke
Rising from the chimney.
Rage sounds like big heavy waves
Crashing against the sea wall.

Tolerance
Tolerance is as yellow as a blossoming flower
On a beautiful summer's day.
Tolerance feels like a relaxing dream
That you don't want to get out of.
Tolerance sounds like a sweet whistle
In the distance.
Tolerance smells like an old-fashioned sweet shop
Making their creamiest chocolate.
Tolerance tastes like the most expensive, yummiest ice cream
In the shop.

Beth Richardson (9)
Valley Gardens Middle School

The Wonderful Season Called Autumn

The windy weather lifting the plants up high.
Then there's also Hallowe'en, everything is scary, even the sky.
Warm clothes come out, and if you wear them
It's like standing in the sun but everybody wants to wear them
Because they're freezing.
'Trick or treat, smell my feet, give me something good to eat,'
That is what they say
And that is autumn.

Oliver Spencer
Valley Gardens Middle School

Autumn Is Fun

Crimson, rosy, crisp, frozen leaves,
Crunchy as I step on the pavement floor.
Crackling as I jump on the growing florid piles.
Trees bare, brown as a bear's coat.

Animals hibernate
Birds migrate
Humans huddle
To escape the colder air.

Festivals are celebrated
Shooting fireworks from rosy bonfires
Shining candles, lighting up for Diwali
Scary Hallowe'en, with monster costumes.
Autumn is here.

Abbie Carr (9)
Valley Gardens Middle School

Autumn Leaves

Crimson gold leaves drifted,
Into a narrow, empty pathway
Fluttering, floating to the cold ground.
Leaving their tree's bare stalk,
Losing their bright autumn colour
The wind picks them up,
They circle gently.
Making patterns in the sky,
Only to fall once more,
Into a huge pile,
Of autumn colour.

Daniel Robertson (9)
Valley Gardens Middle School

Autumn Fever

Trees are bare, leaves are gone.
Crimson, orange, gold, blazing like flames
As they fall, sinking, bobbing to cover
The freezing ground.

Low sun, in the dark sky
Lit by Hallowe'en lanterns
Sparkling fireworks
And Diwali candlelight.

Animals finding warm nests.
Birds searching for the sun
Humans wrapping up snugly
Autumn has arrived.

Johnathon Taylor (10)
Valley Gardens Middle School

Autumn Day

Scarlet, crimson twirling gracefully through the air
Leaves dancing, tumbling to the ground
Crunching and scrunching below my feet.

Bonfires flashing, pink, orange, yellow, scarlet
Filling the dark night sky with twinkling sparks
Crackling, burning, watering my eyes.

Frosty, misty mornings.
Humans, animals try to keep warm.
Extra coats, feathers, fur.

Autumn has arrived.

Laura Campbell (10)
Valley Gardens Middle School

Season Of Autumn

Autumn comes around now
Crimson and amber leaves are falling
On the frosty ground.

Mist vapours around me
As I slip on the frost and ice
Wrapped up against the cold.

Little animals scurry round
Collecting a range of frosted berries
Ready for hibernation.

Some birds fly away
Down south to the warm, beating sun
This is migration.

'Boo!' go small, smiling faces
Hidden under masks and Hallowe'en costumes
Out trick or treating.

Bang! go the fireworks
Coloured like an exploding rainbow
High in the sky.

Autumn comes around now
Leaves are falling and weather is changing
Ready for . . . *winter!*

Imogen Green (9)
Valley Gardens Middle School

Mary

Pink and black,
Rough and patchy,
Round and hairy,
That's my friend Mary,

She doesn't watch her weight,
And wishes she lived near a deli,
Always clears her plate,
I wonder what goes on in her belly,

Potato peelings,
Carrot tops,
Cabbage leaves,
Brussels sprouts,

Yorkshire puddings,
Onion gravy,
Sausage rolls,
She'll eat anything savory,

Jam doughnuts,
Fruity yoghurts,
Ice cream sundaes,
She loves her desserts,

Afterwards she likes to rest,
And wallow in mud up to her chest,
The thought of this may seem scary,
But she's my friend,
Mary.

Dulcie Graham (9)
Valley Gardens Middle School

Autumn Burst

The leaves tumble from the trees drifting from side to side.
The frost dives from the trees on the cold ground
The mist covers the scene.
Scary Hallowe'en nights.
Children getting all the treats.
Share them with your friends and family.
Noisy Bonfire Night.
Fireworks lighting up the dark sky.
Bonfires crackling
Toffee and hot dogs.
Birds searching for the sun.
Animals finding cosy homes for the winter.
Children search out warmer clothes.
Autumn in the air.

Drew Ellen Powell (10)
Valley Gardens Middle School

Leaves

Leaves start falling, drifting down,
To the frozen ground.
The colours are scarlet, crimson, brown.
Freshness of the autumn frost touches the edges.
They leave the trees bare, stripped of
Colours until the spring.
I walk on the slippery ground,
Through misty, cloudy air.
Darkness comes early to the sky.
Autumn surrounds me.

Caroline Taylor (9)
Valley Gardens Middle School

The Autumn

Leaves changing colours,
Crimson, russet, red,
Glowing like the sunshine,
Crunching under feet on
Leaf-coloured ground
Bare withering trees,
Brown, stripped bare.
Mist, fogs and wind, chill
Making humans, birds, animals,
Search for warmth
Spring bulbs hiding underground
Everything hiding
For the coming of winter.
All waiting for the warmth of spring.

James Rowat (9)
Valley Gardens Middle School

Hallowe'en

It's Hallowe'en tonight.
The moon is as bright as a light.
The ghouls and goblins are out tonight.
It's Hallowe'en tonight.

The ghosts are flying high in the sky.
The witch's cat is as black as coal.
The squeals are loud and then they stop.
I'd stay indoors tonight.

Ryan Bird (9)
Valley Gardens Middle School

Autumn

Leaves are changing
Dark nights are coming
Weather getting colder
Autumn's arrived.

Animals hibernate
Birds migrate
Bronze conkers abound
Autumn is here.

Pumpkins carved and lit
Gathering of crops
Fireworks sparkling
Autumn's festivities.
James Robson (9)
Valley Gardens Middle School

The Autumn World

Crimson leaves,
Falling, floating,
Blurring my view,
Crunching noises under my feet
Whooshing fireworks in the night sky.

Animals hibernating,
Birds migrating,
Humans changing into warmer clothes
Searching for warmth
In the autumn world.
Andrew Taylor (10)
Valley Gardens Middle School

Autumn

Celebrations of autumn
Monsters of Hallowe'en
Sparkling fireworks of Bonfire Night
Shining candles at Diwali.

Animals hibernating,
Birds migrating,
Humans wearing warmer clothes
Searching for the warmth of summer.

Swirling, misty mornings,
Icy chill in the air
Dark night skies
Frosty ground.

Autumn is here.

Patrick Maloney (9)
Valley Gardens Middle School

Autumn Is Coming

Crunch . . . crunch went the autumn leaves,
As they crackled under my big boots against the ground.
Rosy red, spicy brown and flaming orange,
Twirling to the frozen floor.
Brrr, the icy cold is in the air,
As the frosty diamonds twinkle in the sky,
While chilly wind wafts about outside,
Wrap up warm, it's freezing cold,
With woolly hats and scarves and mittens to keep our hands warm.

Sophie Hopkins (9)
Valley Gardens Middle School

Emotions Poem

Excitement
Excitement is green like grass
It tastes like chocolate cake
It smells like chocolate
It looks like a phonebooth
It sounds like a sonic screwdriver
It feels like having a ride in the TARDIS.

Boredom
Boredom is grey like water
It tastes like mushrooms
It smells like destructive fire
It looks like a grey zombie's face
It sounds like zombies
It feels like sitting down doing nothing.

Thomas Hoare (9)
Valley Gardens Middle School

Autumn Is Here

Leaves fall on my big black boot.
Crunch, I grind them into the cold ground,
Fireworks shooting off into the dark, misty night sky,
I see shades of crimson, spice and burgundy all around,
Animals rush to hibernate,
Storing winter food,
Birds flying to the sunshine,
Humans putting on extra layers,
Autumn is here.

Eve Beston (9)
Valley Gardens Middle School

Autumn Has Come

Leaves red, orange and russet
Floating, gliding to the frozen ground.
Brown bare trees like empty statues.

Animals, humans, birds searching,
For warmth.
Determined to be cosy and warm.

Festivals, Hallowe'en, Bonfire Night, Diwali
Bring fun, laughter and light,
Into the dark, colder nights.

Autumn has arrived.

Tobias Mill (9)
Valley Gardens Middle School

Fellow Autumn

Crunch went the crimson leaves
Beneath my heavy shoes.
Leaves floating down on top of me
Bare branches hanging over me.
Dark chestnut, brown, yellow and gold.
Animals tuck up nice and warm
Fireworks lighting up the dark night sky.
Celebrations for my birthday.
Autumn is here.

James Glendinning (9)
Valley Gardens Middle School

Hallowe'en

Ghouls and goblins
Witches and ghosts
Creepy-crawlies
Scuttling up posts
Bones and masks
Pumpkins lit up
Drinking blood from a vampire cup
Faces in places
Out in the night
There to scare you and give you a fright
Moans and groans and a scary scream
All of these things on Hallowe'en.

Scott Mogey (9)
Valley Gardens Middle School

Hallowe'en

I'm scared of witches and I'm scared of ghosts
I'm scared of werewolves, spiders and roasts.
I'm scared of blood and I'm scared of thieves,
I'm scared of skeletons, sorrow and grieves.
I'm scared of the pumpkin face though it gives light,
I'm scared of ravens as dark as the night.
I'm scared of wizards and I'm scared of rats,
I'm scared of huge and man-eating bats.
I'm scared of vampires and I'm scared of mice,
I'm getting better though: Hallowe'en is nice!

Hannah Kessler (9)
Valley Gardens Middle School

Fireworks

Zooming fireworks burst
In the air exploding, glowing,
For all that are there.
Guy Fawkes in the bonfire
In he goes and then he's on fire.
Bursting, booming, brightly coloured
Floating past for all that are bothered.
Girl with sparkler eyes so bright,
Glowing gently in the night.
Exploding fireworks ever so light
Lighting up all the night
The fireworks have to go down for the night.

Danielle Rawson (9)
Valley Gardens Middle School

A Crocodile . . .

Swims like a submarine
Smiles like a monster
Has a body as rough as sandpaper
Eyes as black as coal
A tail like a sword
And feet as big as buckets
He moves like lightning
He can disappear like a ghost
And his teeth are as sharp as knives
It's a crocodile.

William Patterson (9)
Valley Gardens Middle School

My Puppy

Wiggles like a worm
Yaps like a fool
Has fur as black as coal
Ears as soft as snow
A tail like a snake
And a nose as wet as water
She plays like a lion
She can jump like a grasshopper
And her teeth are as sharp as pins.

Jonathan Thompson (9)
Valley Gardens Middle School

Star Wars

S tars so bright
T renches so deep
A pples as juicy as your feet
R ivers running to the beat

W ires spiky as lions' teeth
A ir as thin as paper
R oads so bumpy like stairs
S tairs impossible to climb.

Ryan Malarkey (9)
Valley Gardens Middle School

Dogs

Watch out if there is a dog about,
Racing fast the dogs will go,
The dogs are athletes,
Never trust one that's slim and thin,

All sorts of dogs there are,
Different colours and sizes,
You never can tell, young or old,
Blind or not, as cute as ever,

Look at the heart, how good it is,
As cute as ever, it may be a terror,
Dogs doing disastrous deals,
Nobody knows what a dog is like,
Until you have things eaten or not,

Some dogs are 1,000 rabbits as they chew,
Don't put your face too near a good dog or you'll be wet,

Dogs have beautiful coats,
Their coats are as shiny as shoe polish.

Georgina Ross (9)
Valley Gardens Middle School

The Hallowe'en Cat

The Hallowe'en cat said, 'My name is Mister-no-Mat.'
The cats of the street said, 'Why the strange hat?'
'That's no hat,' said the Hallowe'en cat
'That's my friend the Hallowe'en bat!'

The Hallowe'en bat said, 'My name is Rolland Rat,
And I'm the friend of Mister-no-Mat.'
The bats of the street said, 'You are no rat!
You're a bat that is a friend to the Hallowe'en cat!'

Ellie Harkins (9)
Valley Gardens Middle School